A Not Quite
A Geordie Story

This may only be a story but there
is some truth in every story.

James Watson

ISBN 978-1-950818-92-1 (paperback)

Copyright © 2020 by James Watson

All rights reserved. No part of this publication may be reproduced, distributed, or transmitted in any form or by any means, including photocopying, recording, or other electronic or mechanical methods without the prior written permission of the publisher. For permission requests, solicit the publisher via the address below.

Rushmore Press LLC
1 800 460 9188
www.rushmorepress.com

Printed in the United States of America

DEDICATION

This book is for my late wife Heather, who stood by me through some difficult times and as the years roll by without her I realise more and more how much I depended on her and the influence she had and continues to have on our family.

There is no definitive Geordie dialect and there are considerable variations in the speech spoken in Northumberland and Durham. On Tyneside some words and phrases can even differ in meaning depending on whether used in rural or urban districts.

CONTENTS

Dedication 3
Introduction..9
Prologue..11
Chapter 1: The Move...15
Chapter 2: Making Friends and Starting School 26
Chapter 3: Junior School Years 47
Chapter 4: Senior School Years.......................................64
Chapter 5: Final Senior School Year 83
Chapter 6: Art College 107
Chapter 7: Joining the Workforce................................136
Chapter 8: Still Learning the Hard Way 158
Chapter 9: Time to Move On 181
Epilogue...201

INTRODUCTION

I really wanted to write a book, not for ever, have I really wanted to write a book but it seems like as I have gotten older and especially now that I have retired that the desire to write a book has increased. I have always enjoyed reading but I think it is the research that is required as a means of trying to get a book of some sort going that is really the key for me and it can be said that in this present day and age of digital information and internet access nothing should or could be easier. I wonder just how did authors of previous years garner their information before this amazing age of computer technology? Is or was a vivid imagination paramount? Because if that's the case I am behind the eight ball straight off. Or is it necessary to travel the world, documenting everything and everybody? Again, another hurdle for me. What about a college or university education in the arts and a job as a newspaper reporter or reviewer or some sort of artistic critic? Well, there is none of that either, so the challenge is there. I still do not know how those writers of a generation or more ago did it, we have it so much easier now or so it seems. Or maybe that is part of the problem, it is so easy to travel the information highway and because of that there are so many wannabe authors out there but all that does for me is widen and strengthen my admiration of authors of present and previous years. I wonder if I were to write about my own life and experiences then maybe I would not need the imagination or need to be a travel expert but then it probably would not be interesting enough to keep the reader turning the pages, unless I spiced things up a bit. Now there's a thought!

  I have written one book already, published in 2014, a non-fiction effort called 'Religious Thoughts: A Historical Perspective'.

Nothing really new in it except that it contains my thoughts on a particularly controversial subject but there is no intent on my part to sway the reader or even criticise the reader's beliefs or faith. It is more or less a procession of factual statements in a historical format interspersed with my comments and opinions. My only criticism, if that is what it can be called, is to point out that facts cannot be disputed even amongst those who stubbornly continue to bury their heads in the sand. I thought at one time of combining 'Religious Thoughts' with another topic – 'The Middle East', two books in one or possibly making it a separate book but it turned out to be a daunting task, again because of the controversy and the ongoing problems in that part of the world, so the idea was shelved, although there are some unpublished pages stuck in the back of one of my personal copies of 'Religious Thoughts' related to the Middle East topic. Meanwhile I still feel as though I can produce something worthwhile and of interest but this time the attempt will be in the form of a novel, prevailing on my own memories and experiences to add some authenticity to the story and at the same time shed some light on the fortunes and misfortunes of life in the North East of England during a particularly trying time.

One thing has become apparent in my life and that is without humour our lives would be worthless. Humour comes in all shapes and forms and has helped people overcome tremendous obstacles. Humour, not to be confused with frivolity, tasteless jokes or inane TV comedies, allows difficulties to be coped with and maybe a little humour will shine through in the following pages.

Maybe there is a story to tell. Maybe I have a story to tell. But the end result is: what you see is what you get.

PROLOGUE

The North East of England has long had a reputation for toughness. The weather for example, cold winds, rain and snow coming in off the North Sea in the winter, cold winds, rain and snow coming in off the North Sea in the summer, or so it seems sometimes, the main industries – coal mining, ship building, steel making and unemployment all seemed to go hand in hand. But locals flocked to the coastal resorts in the summer with great enjoyment and there were very few complaints about anything. It seemed to be visitors from other parts of the country that did the complaining, well they could always go back to where they came from, couldn't they? None of these visitors could ever complain of the treatment they received from local people either, they were accepted very warmly as a rule. The North East covers a huge area and is divvied up into counties as is the rest of the United Kingdom and a lot of the dividing lines coincide with natural boundaries, rivers usually and there is a real splendid display of ever changing scenery all to be taken advantage of with just a few miles of driving and exploring. Over the last few years, with the closing of the coal mines and the shipyards, emphasis has been on upgrading cities, removing or covering up blots on the landscape like slag heaps and generally trying to attract visitors, both tourists and people looking for permanent employment. Not easy by any means as communities have found out, but one thing the North East does have in abundance is history.

One of the words to come out of the North East and nowhere else in the world is 'Geordie'. The word conjures up all kinds of images and explanations depending who is doing the asking and who is providing the answer. The dictionary says a 'Geordie' is 'a person born or living in or near Newcastle-upon-Tyne', there is no mention of dialect, pronunciation of certain words, nuances related to different areas or accents. The dictionary definition does not even come close to the description of a 'Geordie' so a relatively brief explanation will be attempted here to try and establish a background for the story and the characters.

The dialects of the region take numerous forms such as the Geordie of Tyneside, the Northumbrian dialect, the Wearside dialect of Sunderland and Pitmatic dialect in parts of Durham as well as the south Durham and Teesside accents. The origins of the region's 'language', go back to the end of the fourth century A.D, to a period which signified the end of the Roman occupation in Britain. The departure of the Romans left the local Britons vulnerable to raids by the Picts so they enlisted the help of the Angles and Saxons, a pagan race from over the water in what is now Southern Denmark and Northern Germany. In return for this help and protection the mercenary soldiers were given land. The Angles and Saxons brought with them to Britain a language which was the forerunner of modern English and indeed it was the Angles of Denmark that gave England its name - meaning the Angle land. Over the centuries the old Anglo Saxon language changed beyond recognition with the gradual introduction of Latin, Norman-French and other foreign influences. Today the only part of England where the original Anglo-Saxon language has survived to any great extent is of course the North East. Here the old language survives in a number of varieties, the most notable of which are Northumbrian and Geordie. It is from the ancient Germanic and Scandinavian language of the Angles that the unique local dialects of Northumberland and Durham primarily owe their origins. Distinctively Geordie and Northumbrian words are more than 80 % Angle in origin, compared to standard English, where the figure is less than 30 %. Modern English words by comparison are predominantly of Latin origin because modern English derives from the dialects of southern England which were continuously influenced by the Latin and Norman French. Of course some Geordie words are of more recent origin or are corruptions or words borrowed from other regions, but often the similarities between Anglo-Saxon and

A NOT QUITE A GEORDIE STORY

Geordie can be quite surprising. The Anglo-Saxon 'Northumbrian' dialects of North Eastern England take a number of forms which are often loosely termed 'Geordie' but technically a Geordie can only be a native of those parts of Northumberland and Durham known as Tyneside.

The origin of the word 'Geordie' is more difficult to determine. No-one knows for sure exactly how the residents of Tyneside or perhaps more accurately Newcastle upon Tyne became known as 'Geordies'. One theory is that it was the name given to the workers of the railway pioneer 'Geordie' Stephenson, another is that it was a term for a pitman deriving from the use of Stephenson's 'Geordie' Lamp. Certainly, Geordie was regularly used to describe a pitman during the nineteenth century and during much of the earlier part of the twentieth century it was applied to most natives of the North East. This would seem to support the theory that pitmen were the true Geordies, The most attractive historical explanation for why Newcastle people are called 'Geordies', takes us back to the eighteenth century and the time of the first Jacobite rising which took place in 1715. In the previous year, George I, a German protestant, had been appointed as King of England, Scotland and Wales despite the strong claims of the Catholic James Stuart, who was known as ''The Old Pretender'. George 1's supporters may have been known as 'Geordies'. It is easy to see why people outside the North East often group North Easterners together, as we can identify shared features in the English spoken in the area from the Tees to the border with Scotland. One other comment of note is the different pronunciation of vowels in the Geordie dialect together with the 'sing-song' pattern of speech and the speedy delivery of words, all of which separates the North East from the rest of the United Kingdom.

Just to confuse the issue further, a more recent nickname has appeared, this is the term Mackem and is a name that refers to the accent, dialect and people of the Wearside area, or more specifically Sunderland, a city in North East England. The name Mackem was created when ship workers said we'll mackem and they'll sink em! mackem (mack-em) MAKE THEM, or another phrase was we'll mackem and they'll tackem! (TAKE THEM). There is a difference in the spelling of maybe half a dozen words between Mackem and Geordie, otherwise the two dialects are identical. The difference is in how the words are pronounced and to listen to a Newcastle born person and a Sunderland born person, the difference is like chalk and cheese to a local. Obviously, the word Geordie is more complex than it initially appears and some of the origins of it are lost in time, not that it makes a blind bit of difference to most people, especially those outside of the North East but there have been instances of altercations breaking out during discussions on the subject especially when the participants have had a few pints. A similarity exists with the word 'Cockney' and where the majority of people everywhere assume that 'Cockney' covers everybody from London or the London area, the dictionary states that the word applies to 'a person born in the East End of London, traditionally one born within the sound of 'Bow Bells' (i.e., the bells of St. Mary-le-Bow) and speaking a characteristic dialect'.

Now as it happens, Jimmy was called a 'Geordie' by all and sundry and nobody ever took offence and Jimmy never did insist that he was indeed a 'Geordie' but one day, in a Royal Canadian Legion of all places, some gentleman, a visitor by all accounts, took exception to the fact that Jimmy was being referred to as a 'Geordie', this was after there had been some friendly banter on birthplaces, accents, dialects and such. "You're not a fuckin' Geordie" the visitor stated quite loudly. Well, after a sort of pregnant silence all hell broke loose and eventually, the visitor was returned to his seat. Somehow he had ended up on the floor. His explanation being that a true 'Geordie' was one who was born in a cottage on the banks of the Tyne.

Make of that what you will.

CHAPTER 1

The Move

Eddie Bland was running. Not because it was raining, which it was, actually pouring down, "raining cats and dogs", Eddie thought. He knew that particular saying originated hundreds of years ago when peasants would put their household animals up into the rafters when it rained. Of course when it rained really bad and the houses or hovels being of such a basic construction, these animals would fall from or through the ceiling into the area below. Hence "it's raining cats and dogs". Eddie wondered why he could remember such rubbish and not remember more important things like giving himself more time tonight of all nights. He wasn't running because there was an air raid going on either, which there was, this being Newcastle upon Tyne with all its shipbuilding, docks, armaments factories and coal mines in and around the surrounding area and the fact that it was 1943 and the Germans were notorious for missing their targets especially with their night-time bombing raids or maybe some just jettisoned their bombs without finding their targets. No, he was running because he was late having missed the bus and he wasn't quite sure where the Princess Mary Hospital was and his wife Lizzie was having their second child. Eddie thought, second child, Lizzie was not supposed to have a second child after the birth of Joan six years previous, the doctor had said. Did the doctor say, "make sure you do not have another," or did he say, "you will not be able to have another". Kind of an important thing to remember Eddie thought, not like those bloody cats and dogs. Eddie was not from Newcastle but hailed from eight miles south of the Tyne just off the A1 road in County Durham. In fact, his town had a history going back to the Roman times having being a Roman camp and the name of the town was derived from the old Roman name. Chester-le-Street, as the modern town is known was not a camp by today's thinking but was actually a substantial Roman fort covering just over six acres and was probably called Concangium which was the name of some sort of specialized Roman unit that was garrisoned there. Chester-le-Street did have maternity hospital facilities but the fact that Lizzie may develop some complications, a decision had been made to have her transported to a larger facility in Newcastle. So there he was, just before eight o'clock at night, running in the piss-pouring rain, having just lost his cap under a tram, "better the cap than me" Eddie thought, and there was the hospital just up ahead.

Little Jimmy was born at eight pm and was fine and Lizzie was fine and Eddie was fine because he had just made it in time and Eddie wondered if Joan was okay having been left at the neighbours and he also wondered when he would be able to go back to his shift at the brickyard. No money coming in when you didn't work and money was hard to come by these days. But this job at the brickyard, although physically hard and demanding was better than being down the mine and Lizzie had hated him doing that. So he had left the pit and gone to work shifts at the brickyard and because of the nature of the job it was considered part of the war effort and Eddie was exempt from military call up. He hated that and tried to enlist but they would not let him and so he had to make do with being a member of the Home Guard. Sometimes the Home Guard came under some name calling and scoffing but all in all it was a worthwhile calling. The Bland family lived in a terraced house just off Chester Front Street with no garden and an all concrete backyard that was just big enough for the dustbin and the front door opened right onto the street plus the house was too close to the main Front Street traffic for their liking so Eddie and Lizzie put their names down for a new council house just a little way out of town, up Pelaw Bank as it happens, close to South Pelaw Colliery. In fact their names had been down for a good length of time as these council houses were in great demand although in some ways where they lived was handy being in Chester and close to everything, but it did have its drawbacks especially when Jimmy disappeared one day. He was four years old and this independence and challenge of authority was to keep raising its head over the years but this was early days as they say. Well, there is nothing worse for parents than when their kid disappears and little Jimmy had wandered off somewhere. Not only had he wandered off but it became apparent that he may have crossed over the Front Street and if that was the case then he may have wandered down towards the river. The reason why this thought had entered the minds of Eddie and Lizzie was that a short while ago they had all taken a walk down to the river where there was a nice park and some kids' swings and a roundabout, which the kids called a 'tea pot lid' and a slide and the like and Jimmy had loved it and created quite a scene when it was time to come home. He particularly liked the 'tea pot lid' and it was just as well Eddie had to hold him when he went on as he was too small to ride by himself, so he had to come off when Eddie decided it was time to come off. Later-on when he was older and big enough to go on by himself he would ride it but then he had an awful experience one time when some big kids came along and started spinning it really fast and he wanted them to stop but they just laughed and sent it spinning even faster until some adults eventually brought the incident to a welcome end. Jimmy never ever went on the 'tea pot lid' again, the incident created a distrust of all fairground rides for the rest of his life but he didn't tell anyone about it. When it was accepted that Jimmy had disappeared the police were called and of course the whole neighborhood was helping in the search because everybody knew everybody else around there at that time and everybody knew everybody else's business and it was a good thing they did because it lessened the chance of some stranger coming around and doing awful things. The day wore on and panic was close to setting in when little Jimmy was spotted just toddling back home attempting to cross back over the busy high street and demanding to know what all the fuss was about just because he had decided to go for a walk.

Another good aspect of where they lived was that Jimmy was close to a nursery school which was located just around the corner next to Atkinson's Bus Garage, he loved that and Lizzie was able to keep her job going at Horner's Toffee factory where they made the world famous Dainty Dinah toffees. Italian families had moved into the North East which was good for business and sure enough there were a couple of Italian businesses nearby, in fact a couple of streets up from their Albert Street house, towards the railway was the ice cream factory run by the Citrone family or was it the Staffiery family? Eddie could never figure that one out but anyway their ice cream was absolutely delicious, the rumour was they were into other stuff as well but nobody gave a shit in those days. It was only when the 'do gooders' came along and ruined it for everybody that people realized what they had missed and what had been good for the area all that time. So there were obviously some things to give up and decisions to be made, if and when they were to get their council house. There were no more serious incidents with Jimmy going missing or stuff like that but there was one thing at least they were going to miss and that was the bread and cakes and even just the aroma that came from the baker's shop just around the corner. This was Denison's and Mr. Denison made the best ever meat and potato pasty in the world and later on Jimmy would forever go out of his way to walk up to the shop and buy some. This was also an excuse to look at the old neighbourhood, especially Albert Street and for quite some time after they moved there were still old friends there and visiting them remained a special occasion. Jimmy never really thought about it until years afterwards but he had an Auntie Dora and Uncle Ronnie in one street and an Auntie Eva and Uncle Fred in another and some Auntie and Uncle in another and Jimmy always, even later on when he was much older, referred to them as Auntie and Uncle. But of course they were not true blood relatives, the Auntie and Uncle bit was just the way it was in those days to refer to those special friends. Eddie and Lizzie always used to say, "let's go to Auntie Dora's," or "Auntie Eva's coming to visit," and so it went on year after year. Small wonder Jimmy was confused about family matters because there were indeed some real Aunts and Uncles around. Anyway there was no confusion in Jimmy's mind at that time, just, "can I go out to play now?" or, "do I really have to come in now?" seemed to be all that mattered to him.

Those war years were hard for everybody in the country and for the North East in particular but the war created employment and when the war ended in 1945 it wasn't just a case of going back to the way things were, for one thing there was a huge shortage of necessities and food rationing was imposed. In 1947 they moved into their new council house and were delighted with what they got, a three-bedroomed semi with a good sized garden at the back and a small garden at the front. The house was so new, the workmen were still building further down the street and it was a problem keeping the little kids from walking in the wet cement. The kids seemed to think that because they were wearing wellies[1] they could walk anywhere. Building sites at that time were not as restricted or patrolled as they maybe should have been. One such incident involved the little girl who lived next door to the Bland's where she had gone toddling off down the street and onto a newly cemented footpath. There erupted such a torrent of shouting and cursing that the poor girl started bawling her eyes out and just stood there, frozen or cemented to the spot, one might say. Eventually someone yelled, "you had better get her off there before the bloody stuff sets," and of course that section of footpath had to be re-done. One of the few downsides at the new location was that Joan was going to school in Chester which was now some distance away and the same for Eddie who had a longer bus ride to the brickyard and Jimmy was not able to go to the same nursery beside the bus garage and Lizzie had to find some other way to get to the toffee factory. There were jobs to be had in Chester, but for the men, most of the available work was in the coal mines, of which there were quite a number within a short radius of the town. There were a fortunate few who lived at South Pelaw who had been able to get work at South Pelaw Colliery or had been able to transfer there. Long before the council houses were built, there were already colliery row houses dating back 100 years with colliery management

---

[1] Wellie – Wellington boot

houses up near the pit and all these were still fully occupied. In fact all the jobs were in the Chester unless you happened to be a coal miner working at South Pelaw Colliery which was just up the road from their new council house or the coke works which was just a bit further away which used to stink when they were burning off the gas and depending on which way the wind was blowing. Eddie loved the idea of having a garden, he neither smoked nor drank so this was something he could get his mind into and get his hands dirty. A lot of his work mates smoked and drank a bit but he wasn't interested, he did miss playing football with the lads though, which he had done right up until getting married. He had played center half and although he wasn't very tall for that position he was quite strong so he did alright and he was appreciated by his mates but things change when you get married, adjustments have to be made and lifestyles need to be prioritized but it doesn't mean the end of the world does it? Well, it might for some unfortunately, but not for Eddie. It seems strange that Eddie was kind of quiet and more than a little on the nervous side, not timid mind you, just a little tentative with some things, not the sort of characteristics normally associated with a chap who had played football, which was no softies game and done physical work with rough, tough physical men but this nervousness got to the stage at one point where Lizzie suggested he go and see the doctor about it. Well, that suggestion didn't go down too well as Eddie remarked, "real men don't go to the doctors for stuff like that, it's like going to the doctors with a hangnail or a spelk[2] in your finger or a bloody headache," but he went anyway. Of course doctors ask all sorts of personal things, things normal people don't usually talk about but they have to do that if they are to get at the root of the problem, if there is one. There was nothing physically wrong with Eddie, that much was obvious and at the end of the chat and examination the doctor asked Eddie if he had ever thought about smoking. Eddie hadn't but he could not help thinking of the joke –

"Do you smoke after intercourse"?

---

[2] spelk – a small wooden splinter or sliver

"I don't know I never looked", and Eddie must have allowed a little smile to appear because the doctor got annoyed and told Eddie it was no laughing matter. Well, Eddie couldn't very well tell the joke to the doctor so he had to apologize and agreed that it was indeed no laughing matter. The doctor explained that in some cases nicotine in the cigarette had a calming and soothing effect and may help in Eddie's situation. So from that day Eddie smoked, not a lot to be sure as it was an additional expense and in fact he turned to smoking a pipe in later years but it did help a bit except that his clothes had a different smell now as Lizzie noticed and remarked upon.

Lizzie was a lot happier now because life had not been too kind to her up to that point, her father had been a wife abuser and a drunk and had been responsible for her mother's death during an unwanted pregnancy and childbirth which had resulted in Lizzie and her brother being removed from their house and put into a children's care facility which was just a workhouse for abandoned and unwanted children and un-wed mothers and generally those places were just awful. Because of this poor upbringing her brother was already in trouble with the police and as soon as war broke out in 1939 he enlisted in the army. Lizzie still had Walter's last letter where he had said he would not be coming home as there was nothing for him there and he would just end up in jail. He didn't come home. He was killed in action in Tobruk in North Africa. Years later Lizzie was stopped in the Street by a friend from way back and told that her father had died and Lizzie, who did not have an unkind word to say about anybody, despite everything, felt nothing, absolutely nothing, remembering only the bad times caused by this man. Jimmie's parents were both small in stature but to him and Joan they were big and as tough as nails, maybe it was just the way life was in the North East or maybe the war hardened them but both kids knew that their parents were not to be messed with and to expect punishment when they did wrong. Even Joan, who was not very big either and who had had some difficult early months as a baby knew not to expect any favours. Shortly after she was born her eyesight had been such a concern that both eyes had to be covered for months which resulted in her wearing glasses from an early age and this is a real hardship to accept for boys and girls.

Jimmy was four years old in 1947 when the family moved house and he wasn't a sickly child by any means but being a war baby meant that he and his mother had been deprived of some nourishments especially those dairy foods which contained calcium and those dairy foods were still in short supply just after the war and families were still required to produce ration books and stamps to get them. Calcium is necessary for strong teeth and bones and the lack of it is noticeable in white streaks in finger nails and poor looking teeth and so it was with Jimmy, he was average weight and height by this time but looked a bit pasty faced and a few more pounds on his frame wouldn't have gone amiss. Not only were dairy foods in short supply but there had already been occasions in their new house when there was no water and family members had to take their buckets to the tap up the road which was guarded by some Gestapo looking individual who seemed to have found his true niche in life. But the house was nice, it had a coal burning stove in the kitchen which also heated the water and a coal burning fireplace in the front room and coal was available, at a cost, unless you worked at the pit. In time Eddie got to know Jack around the corner who worked at the pit and delivered coal in his lorry and he would let Eddie have a load which had to be transported by wheelbarrow from Jack's house to Eddie's, usually at night because it could've cost Jack his job. Later, Jimmy used to hate these episodes because he was to do the transporting as the coal just couldn't be left lying around. It had to be tossed into the coalhouse where Eddie had installed wooden slats across the front which could be inserted or removed depending on how much coal was in there. Well, as the coal house filled up Jimmy could hardly reach up and over the top slats and usually ended with coal and coal dust all over the yard which still had to be cleaned up somehow and he ended up looking like one of those Black and White Minstrels he had seen pictures of.

So South Pelaw became their new home, or just Pelaw as everybody called it, not to be mistaken for the other Pelaw near Gateshead beside the River Tyne. And everybody referred to Chester-le Street as Chester or the just the Street and it was good,

A NOT QUITE A GEORDIE STORY

new friends were made and old friends came to visit from time to time. When Eddie walked down to Chester, which was often, he had to walk down Pelaw Bank and he never got tired of the view from the railway bridge, this bridge was over the main London to Edinburgh railway and the view was down into the town itself with the River Wear in the background and Lumley Castle sitting majestically as it had done for centuries. The origins of Lumley Castle date back to the ninth century and although the castle, as seen today was constructed in the fourteenth century, with some additions over the years, its name originates with Sir Ralph Lumley who was a well-known figure at that time. In 1389 he was captured by the Scots after playing a key role in the defence of Berwick-on-Tweed and imprisoned and on his return petitioned the Bishop of Durham to allow him to convert the manor house built by his ancestors into a castle. Later, unfortunately, he was involved in a conspiracy to overthrow Henry IV, a coup that failed and which led to the arrest of Sir Ralph and his son Thomas, they were stripped of their titles and eventually executed in 1400. The land and wealth belonging to the Lumley family was given to the Earl of Somerset but after his death, having no family to bequeath his inheritance to, under Elizabethan law, the land was restored to its rightful owners, in this case Sir Ralph's grandson Thomas. Eddie had made it his business to learn a little history of the area because his family were from the village of Lumley and he had got a job working for Lumley Brickworks and he was truly amazed and surprised at the amount of local history to be found if you had a mind to look for it. He wondered if his brother and sisters ever took the time to find out the history of the area but it seemed to Eddie that all they wanted was to get out of there, which they did eventually, moving south, getting married and getting a better life, or so they hoped. But they all kept in touch and there was the occasional visit.

Lumley Castle was not the only castle in the area either but it certainly looked like a proper castle and was even reputed to be haunted which perked up Jimmie's interest and he found it fascinating especially the way his dad told the story. Lambton Castle was more of a recent structure with modern add-ons and the like and where the Lumley family tradition had been mainly of a soldierly nature, the

Lambton family name, although with centuries of tradition, meaning land and royalty connections, there had also been considerable military achievements. The Lumley ancestral name went way back and was linked to the area whereas the Lambton lands, although linked with Lambton village and the Lambton pits had been acquired from the Hedworth and D'Arcy families in part through marriage. In fact, present day Lambton Castle stands on the site of Harraton Hall, and old mansion of the D'Arcy's which, unfortunately, partially collapsed in 1854 because of old, long forgotten mine workings underneath and resulted in the place being partly restored and partly rebuilt with the castle proper being built about 1820. Harraton Hall had been in the Hedworth family since the early 15th century but in 1696 Dorothy Hedworth, heiress to the Hedworh Estate married Ralph Lambton and so the property passed into the Lambton hands. The Lambton family eventually moved to Biddick Hall, a smaller, elegant place on the estate but the castle remained the ancestral home on the 1500 acre estate. "Here I go again", Eddie thought, thinking history. But that's okay as long it doesn't become a pre-occupation but he did surprise himself sometimes with his knowledge of the area and he made up his mind to pass this knowledge on to little Jimmy whenever he got the chance. Never seemed to have that chance with Joan or maybe Joan never showed the same interest. He suddenly found himself singing the old Lambton Worm chorus:

> "Whisht! lads, haad ya gobs,
> Aa'll tell ye aall an aaful story,
> Whisht! lads, haad ya gobs,
> An aa'll tell ye 'boot the worm."

And he thought, "bloody hell's bells, get a grip, you've got work to do, been day dreamin' a bit too much lately". But all this history thinking and especially the Lambton's, did remind him of the story of the Lambton Worm and it was supposedly John Lambton, the heir to the estate, maybe as far back as the 14th century who fought this creature one Sunday when he should have been at church but he had gone fishing in the Wear instead. Anyway the church or chapel referred to in the story as Eddie had read, was located on Newbridge Bank near the bridge just inside the entrance to Lambton Park and was known as Brugeford in those days. Well, Eddie had been flabbergasted when he had read this because he had walked up and down Newbridge Bank many times and had thought that what he was looking at were the ruins of some cottage or other, which may still have been the case but the ruins of Brugeford Chapel had stayed identifiable for many years. And all this thinking about pits and stuff made Eddie wonder if anybody had any idea, a drawing maybe, of all the mine workings underground, because the area must be riddled with tunnels. He had seen a bit of paper which listed eighty-seven pits or drifts, not just the Lambton pits mind you but those ones up at Craghead and Waldridge and Sacriston and all around Chester. Maybe the whole North East is just ready to collapse in on itself at any time, he thought. This sort of stuff was much more interesting than the stuff they threw at you at school, the only thing the teachers seemed to be interested in were the three R's. Reading, Riting and Rithmetic, no wonder kids didn't want to go to school. He did acknowledge the schooling was better now than when he went and Joan was doing really well at Chester Modern and Jimmy would eventually go to Pelton where there were Infant, Junior and Senior schools all together but he would have to leave at fifteen years old unless he passed the eleven plus which would allow him to go to Chester Grammar School.

CHAPTER 2

Making Friends and Starting School

Jimmy missed his friends in Chester but there were new ones to be made and new places to discover and explore but it wasn't going to be all play for him as his Mam was making every effort to teach him to read, because even at his early age she realised the importance of books and the knowledge to be gained from them and of course Eddie was all for it as well. Fortunately, Jimmy was into this reading thing and would spend hours just looking at pictures without fully understanding the captions and words beside them but that would change soon enough. Although theirs was a new council house, there were other, older houses up at Pelaw, some on the main road up to Pelton, which had been built for the miners originally, with a separate row of terraced houses for the mining officials up near the pit, but there were other houses near-by whose occupants were named by the new lads as the 'Top Enders', who didn't seem to take too kindly to these new folk moving onto their turf. This was to be the cause of many a conflict over the years, especially November the fifth – 'Bonfire Night' or 'Guy Fawkes' as it is officially known and the days or in some cases weeks leading up to that night. Everyone knows the story of Guy Fawkes, he was eventually branded as a traitor for his attempt to blow up the Houses of Parliament in London in 1605. It was the accidental discovery of his explosives that failed the attempt but his name went into the history books nevertheless and each November the fifth bonfires are built and lit and fireworks are set-off to commemorate the event. No doubt there have been some wishful 'Guy Fawkes' since then. Around Jimmy's estate there was very little wood with which to build a decent size 'bonny' as the lads called it so they would cut down and drag branches and anything else that would burn from the nearest wooded area, which happened to be the same wood that Jimmy and his pals were forbidden to visit. The 'Top Enders' would build their 'bonny' and the 'Bottom Enders' would build their 'bonny' and rival gangs would attempt to steal from each other, which led to all kind of fights. Most adults took the position 'that boys will be boys' but there were some big lads, almost men, on either side and the fights would continue into the school time, gathering momentum and support from those who just wanted to fight and didn't need a reason.

The Bland's house was on one of the longer streets, built on quite a slope, which eventually would also be part of the bus route but more importantly it was ideal for sledging down, not that they always got enough snow for tobogganing but when they did it was great and the kitchen stove top was also great for drying out his soggy mittens and socks. The local bobby lived at the top of the street, near the main road and this was always to be known as the 'copper's house' and to be steered clear from but in time all the lads got to know him quite well for one reason or another. Jimmy's bedroom faced north onto the street and he could look over to the pit heap and see and hear the railway engines shunting the wagons backwards and forwards all day and all night dropping their loads of stone and slag which sometimes were still smouldering and this would create quite a hazard which was why the pit heap was off bounds especially to inquisitive kids. Can you imagine how attractive that was to the young'uns? And off in the distance he could see the chimneys at the coke works especially at night when the flames would light up the sky, but more interesting was what was right in front of him between the road and the pit heap. This was a large fenced off area where a number of buildings shaped something like aircraft hangars[3] and there were signs all over the place saying 'Keep Out' and 'No Trespassing', well this was like waving a red a flag at a bull but these potential explorations for Jimmy and his mates were to come much later.

The next summer, Jimmy contracted Scarlet Fever which put him in the local Isolation Hospital for six weeks and any possessions he decided to take for the duration of his stay would not be allowed to be returned home with him so obviously he didn't want to take anything. When the reasons were explained to him he finally seemed to understand but that didn't mean he accepted the conditions. The ambulance came and the neighbours gawked and little Jimmy was just carried out like a sack of potatoes, but more carefully. He cried because he didn't fully understand what was going on, he only knew that the sun was shining, the sky was blue and he just wanted to be outside playing. He took a book, not knowing if they would have any books and a clip-on comb that could be attached to his coat or shirt pocket, which was one of his prized possessions and he figured he could hide it when the time came to come home. He had blond, curly hair and lots of it and was forever trying to comb out the curls 'cos he thought they made him look like a girl. Some of the stubbornness and resistance to authority which was to become evident later-on was beginning show itself and he was learning and would continue to learn that to beat authority he would just have to be smarter which turned out to be very seldom the case and in most cases people were just trying to help him but he seemed to think he was displaying weakness by accepting help. The hospital stay was quite uneventful, there were some other kids there but being in isolation they didn't get to see much of anything other than those who were in the same

---

[3] These were Bevin Boys' Huts, named after Ernest Bevin, then Minister of Labour and National Service who recruited 48,000 young men, some were volunteers but most were conscripts, to replace a shortage of wartime coal miners who had left the pits to join up and fight. The programme ran from 1943 until 1948 and the boys received no medals, nor were they given the right to jobs they held previously (unlike armed forces personnel) and were not fully recognized as contributors to the war effort until 1995.

ward and Jimmy couldn't wait to being 'let out', as he put it. Lizzie picked him up at the hospital when it was time to leave and she brought him some clothes and a new pair of boots, black boots with studs in the soles and his eyes lit up when he saw them. They had a bit of a walk to get home but that was okay, it was a nice day but Jimmy just stopped suddenly and blurted out, "mam aa cannot walk, me leg hurts bad," and sure enough as Lizzie watched he struggled to even limp along, hardly using his right leg. Lizzie had been told there could be some temporary after effects which would wear off in time but she never expected anything like this and it was breaking her heart to see him struggle with the tears almost flowing again. She decided to wait for a bus rather than force Jimmy to walk although walking and exercise may have been the better thing to do, just to try and get the leg moving again. That leg continued to be a problem for some time and although it continued to improve it was never quite 100% again but the limp was hardly noticeable, more a kind of unnatural leg movement especially when he was hurrying but it never hindered his ability to run and play and eventually play football with some skill. He never did get his comb back or his book but he had learned some card games and he could shuffle cards better than most adults, not that that was a skill he would be encouraged to keep or display when applying for a job.

    Soon it was time to start school, at age five kids went into the Infant school, at age seven into the Junior school and at age eleven into the Senior school, all depending on just what month your birthday fell. So Jimmy went into the Infants, Joan was now eleven and was at the senior level at her school in Chester and was doing quite well. Lizzie had sent her for Scottish Dancing and piano lessons at no small cost either but Eddie's work was steady days now, not the shiftwork he had done for years. Things seemed to be moving along well, considering the end of the war was just a little-ways back, ration books and stamps were gradually being phased out and Lizzie had an account number at the large Cooperative store in Chester which allowed her to get some things on tick which she very rarely did. Years later, when Jimmy was into his early teens he stumbled across his mam's store account number and he memorized it for future use.

He didn't go overboard with the use of it but he did not tell his mam either and he would only look on innocently when he would overhear her telling Eddie, "the store has made a mistake again." But things came to a head when he started smoking and was putting his cigarettes on his mother's account. Eventually he owned up and there was hell to pay and he felt pretty guilty that he had allowed things to get out of hand because not getting into debt and buying only when they could afford had been drummed into the Bland kids from an early age, probably as a result of wartime experiences.

Jimmy was into his second year at the Infants school when the dicky[4] nurse made a visit and this was always a huge event for the kids as they made fun of everybody who was going in to be tested and even those who were coming out after being tested. Mind you for little'uns this could be an unnerving experience as the medical people used some kind of large lamp and did some poking around. Kids can be and were so cruel and at that time dicks and lops[5] were a common occurrence amongst school children but usually there were never any cases at Jimmy's school. Well, the bombshell dropped, Jimmy and a neighbour's kid had a problem which was diagnosed as 'Ringworm'. This was a disaster, not just for the families involved, who had to deal with the associated stigma but the kids in the class as well and Jimmy who, although sometimes spoke his piece was somewhat shy and sensitive to personal things and he took this hard, not to mention the schooling he would lose while he underwent treatment. Ringworm was very contagious and he had to be removed from the school immediately and the burden of looking after him while he was off school fell to Lizzie who had to leave work to be able to do that. The other problem was that Jimmy was still fully fit and active otherwise and as with the scarlet fever episode, he did not fully understand the significance of his ailment, so how do you keep a child occupied all day and every day? Lizzie realized more than anybody how important these early schooling years were and she never bowed under the

---

[4] The dicky nurse was a medical practitioner who would look for head lice and other scalp and hair infections.

[5] Lops were an infestation of the skin associated with uncleanliness.

enormous workload and pressure and tried to continue with his education as best she could but especially his reading skills which already were advanced for his age. Even so she needed a break sometimes and as it was summer she would get him on a bus and take him to the seaside and he loved that and the coast always had that attraction for him. Maybe it was inborn or because of those excursions but he was fascinated forever afterwards by the sea and the waves and the sand and the cold didn't seem to bother him that much. Part of the early treatment for his ringworm was the removal of all his hair, Lizzie and Joan just wept at their first sight of Jimmy without his hair, all that lovely blond curly hair that girls would just die for, gone forever, but they bought him a cap which prevented some of the nasty comments that some people seem to take a delight in making. What is it with these people? How about showing some compassion? All Jimmy knew was that he seemed to be off school an awful long time, nine months to be exact, he found out later, and when he did go back he was another year older and was enrolled in the Junior school, so gone was his Infants school career and memories. Lizzie and Eddie fretted and worried what sort of effect all this missed schooling would have on his future education and even his eventual working career but his future options would be determined by how he approached his present predicament wouldn't it? And as far as he was concerned it was not the missed schooling that was the immediate problem, it was being picked on all the time by certain kids because of his lack of hair and the cap that he was permitted to wear in the classroom and outside of course, which seemed to be a magnet for all sorts of name calling. Bullying is the term for this type of behaviour and Eddie had told him a while back that going to school was not just about learning from books, which was tremendously important, but learning how to deal with situations, not all situations would be pleasant either and he would meet boys who were different than he was and some would not be too interested in school or learning at all. Some boys would be just downright nasty and there would always be one in every school who was just a big bully and this type of boy wouldn't cause trouble on his own because underneath his big show, he was a coward and he always had a couple of pals to back him up.

His dad had told him he would have to learn when to walk away and just let the taunts go right over his head but there would be times when he would have to stand on his own two feet and give back as much as he took whatever the consequences and he would find that usually if he did this then the bully would stop bothering him. Unbeknownst to his parents Jimmy had already had run-ins with a boy in the school yard who had seen the small framed lad as a soft touch and this boy was not from the same housing estate but was from up near the school somewhere and Jimmy had spotted him straight off as trouble and whenever he saw him, either in the school yard before or after school he attempted to dodge him, but he knew that could not go on indefinitely. This kid always wore the same clothes, no matter the weather and always looked scruffy, he had a kind of grey woollen polo necked jersey which had new holes coming through faster than the old holes could be darned and a pair of brown corduroy trousers which looked like they had been slept in and which stunk of dried piss. Kids were not allowed into the school building before opening bell and when it was raining there was a large open ended shed down one wall of the playground with the side opposite the wall open and a roof which provided some cover from the weather and there were a few bench seats and the kids would play marbles or toss cigarette cards until it was time to go in. The school yard had a bit of a slope to it from the wall of the classrooms on one side down to the outside toilets and this was ideal for making slides when it was icy underfoot and Jimmy's boots were just the ticket for doing the sliding, providing he could keep his balance and providing his leg didn't give out which was still a bit weak. This was the set-up then at the junior school and if it hadn't been for this troublesome kid bothering him he would be enjoying school life but there had already been a few incidents and it was all very well his Mam telling him to report all this to the teacher when he had mentioned it to her one day, "yeah right, go running to the teacher like a wimp", Jimmy thought, "that would make matters worse not better". One awful, dreary rainy morning, most of the kids, including Jimmy, were taking shelter under the shed roof waiting for the opening school bell to ring when he espied the bully boy together with his two cronies, making their way straight towards him. Well, Jimmy thought, it was bound to happen sooner or later wasn't it? He wasn't thinking of what his dad had said to him or what his mam had said for that matter, in fact he wasn't thinking about anything other than he suddenly wanted to go to the toilet and he wished the ground under him would just swallow him up and everything would be fine. Isn't it strange how kids suddenly know what is going on because the crowd in front of Jimmy just opened up to let the bully boys through and there Jimmy stood, on his tod[6] as usual. The bully shot out his hand and knocked his cap off and into the dirt while his buddies giggled like little girls. Jimmy picked up his cap and placed it back on his head, "gonna run to the teacher are yer?, well aa'll see about that," bully smirked. Bully stepped forward to hit Jimmy on the head again and as he did so, Jimmy just hauled back and smacked him right on the schnoz. Talk about a look of surprise and disbelief, there was all that and more on bully's face and he was blinking furiously trying to clear his eyes from the tears that were welling up and blurring his vision when Jimmy hit him again, right on the same spot, this time there was not just tears but a bit of blood started to trickle down bully's chin. "D'yer think aam just gonna stand here and let yer walk aall ower me, you smelly arsed piece of shit," said Jimmy quietly. The bell went and Jimmy walked away, he was as white as a sheet and shaking like a leaf and he thought to himself, I'm in real trouble now. The teachers at the school usually had one member allocated for yard duty during recesses but obviously not before school start in the mornings or after school hours but they did know what was going on and bully boy's antics had been well noted long before Jimmy's incidents as there was always some willing student who maybe sought to gain favour by tale telling and of course Jimmy's predicament and circumstances were known to the teachers and head mistress Miss Wheeler. So, unknown to Jimmy, the fight episode had been duly noted by the authorities and bully boy was subsequently summoned to the office and warned that any future occurrence would result in his expulsion. As far as Jimmy was concerned and as time went on

---

[6] tod – North East slang for being on your own.

and nothing happened and bully boy never bothered him again, he realised that his dad was right (and weren't dads always right?) about what he had said about standing up for yourself sometimes. Jimmy was never going to say anything about what had happened but he had a feeling his dad knew there had been a growing up episode of some sort, maybe Jimmy stood taller or put his shoulders back or did something but there had been a change and Lizzie remarked to Eddie once, "he seems different now somehow."

Well, the school system, being as archaic and unbending as school systems usually are, had put Jimmy in the 'B' class on his return to school after the ringworm problem, there being an 'A' and 'B' system of classes all the way through the Pelton school system. Made sense in a way, how is the school to know where to put any child? There has to be some evaluation procedure, based on what though? Sports ability? neatness of dress? manners?, knowing the answer to two plus two? What? Not so straightforward as it seems is it? It had been a couple of weeks since the incident with bully boy and the second class of the morning for Jimmy that day was English and this particular day was no different from any other school day in that they all seemed long and all he wanted to do was get out and play football while there was still enough light and even then he would play under the street lights. This part of the English lesson was individual reading and Jimmy just hated being singled out in anything even though he was okay at reading. His desk was about in the middle to back of the class and he could see the clock and there were about forty-five kids in the class and it looked like Mrs. Lee, the teacher, had started at the front as was systematically going desk to desk, row to row, so he was busy trying to work out if the bell would go before his turn came when he realised that all was quiet and he heard, "James, are you with us?" He hadn't even been following the book's progress, heck, he didn't know which page they were on and it was his turn to read. His face was burning as he stood up, the teacher politely suggesting he turn to page sixty-three and read out loud the following four paragraphs, which amounted to about three pages and which no one else in the class that morning had been required to read as much. He could feel all eyes on him and he could even hear a few sniggers and he thought" I'd rather be smacking bully boy on the schnoz right now than this" but he found the page and the paragraph and he started to read. He had not read this book before and he stumbled a bit at first but then his confidence came through and he just read and read until eventually Mrs. Lee said, "alright James, thank you, that's enough."

The following day Jimmy was in the 'A' stream class. At first he wasn't sure what was happening but at the first opportunity Mrs. Boyd, the 'A' class teacher, explained that whilst it was highly unusual, the Head Mistress had felt that, with the recommendation of Mrs. Lee, Jimmy should be moved up on the strength of his reading ability. Mrs. Boyd also added that this arrangement could be reversed, as if to put a damper on the situation. Jimmy's hair was gradually returning, not the blond curly stuff he was glad to note but a nice fair colour was coming in and with the return of the hair came some confidence and soon he wasn't wearing the cap at all. It is a remarkable thing, confidence, a person can be overconfident, resulting in a swaggering overbearing attitude or lacking any confidence, making it difficult to get out of bed on a morning so it is important to try and establish the right balance. All sorts of things effect confidence, physical size, or lack of it, physical disability, inability to stay focused on something important, a seemingly mental block preventing learning something relatively simple or just an inbred shyness that will forever remain an issue. All these facts can be apparent in school children and not all school teachers have the skills nor the patience to deal with the issues, nor, it can be argued, should they be required to. A teacher's job is to teach and educate the pupil in whatever the subject happens to be and in the appropriate age group and if the pupil has an obvious learning impediment then that should be dealt with by an experienced professional. But, you would think, some responsibility should be borne by the teacher and for the most part, a teacher would certainly accept this responsibility and challenge. Alas, in the real world..................

Jimmy loved the fine weather and he would be out and about for as long as he thought he could get away with it and he would play for hours on his own, with a ball, any size ball, even a tennis ball, in his back yard, just as he sometimes watched Alan, down the street, doing exactly the same (but Alan was to go on and become a top class professional footballer). Keeping the ball in the air, head, feet, chest – no hands – off the wall, backwards and forwards, up and down, counting, trying to beat his previously established record. Other times the lads would get together and form two teams and play against each other over on the field beside the pit heap. They would play until it was too dark to see the goalposts which were just piles of cast off coats and jumpers[7] or until enough mothers called for supper and there were not enough players left for two teams. When he got a bit older and could stay out later, the lads and he had developed a game which they called 'Gatesy'. The next street to Jimmy's was a cul-de-sac and the way the semis were built, each had its own front garden and garden gate. The gate was wrought iron and had a latched closing handle and all the gates were connected by a low brick wall. Each lad would select a gate and this would be his goal, he had to stop the other lads from scoring on his goal while he tried to score on any of theirs. They would play for hours, the street lights would come on and they would still by playing and the lads were all pretty good players so the ball would be kept low but there was always a chance of a mishap, and there was always a concerned neighbour, concerned for his garden maybe, for his car maybe, if he had one, or his front window or maybe he was just a prick. In any event, sometimes the local constable would suddenly appear, sweeping down on his bicycle, not very visible because it was kind of dark and his uniform was dark to match so the lads would scatter and take pot luck 'cos the bobby couldn't catch everybody and the backs of the houses were such that you could run down a connecting path and be in your own house in next to no time. Well, this particular time, Jimmy made it home in record time, coat off, grabbing something to eat, sweating like a pig though, when a knock came to the back door. Lizzie and Jimmy were in the kitchen at the time and the back door had a frosted glass panel at the top so you could kind of make out the shape with the moonlight behind, and

---

[7] Jumper-slang for sweater.

the shape was huge and there was no mistaking the shape of a bobby's helmet sitting on top of an enormous bobby's head. Lizzie looked at Jimmy, "have you been playing football in the street again?" she asked. Jimmy just shook his head, "no mam," he said. Lizzie had a dread of the police, not policemen themselves, who she admired but she figured that if a policeman was at her house then something was terribly wrong. Lizzie opened the door and this giant figure stood there, giant to Jimmy and giant especially to Lizzie who was only four feet eleven and the giant had a ball in his hands. "Is this ball yours Jimmy?" the policeman enquired. "No sir," said Jimmy, feeling quite chuffed because he had called the behemoth bobby, sir and thinking that would go down well in his defence. "Well how come it's got you name on it then," the bobby replied. Jimmy could think of nothing to say except he had seen a movie once where the robber was nabbed and he had said, "okay. Guv, it's a fair cop," but he thought maybe he was in enough trouble already. Lizzie was making profound excuses for her son's behaviour, almost grovelling Jimmy thought and making silly statements like she would make sure it would not happen again.

All this footballing was paying off with Jimmy, he was quite skillful with the ball and could run, although his leg still bothered him occasionally and he could still have used a few more pounds just to fill him out a bit. He ate well but maybe he was just going to be one of those kids who never put on a lot of weight. He was in the second year of the Junior school now and his form teacher, Mr. Hutchison, who was also the PE and games teacher, along with the help of another older male teacher, was trying to put together a football team. The junior school, up to that point had not seen it as a priority to have such a thing as a boys' football team. Probably because it was run by a Head Mistress and most of the teachers were women, Jimmy thought, but it was a new idea and quite a challenge. There were try-outs and competitions and make shift games on the field, which belonged to the senior school, as they did have a football team, "probably because they had a Head Master", Jimmy thought when things slowed down a bit so that he could think about some things. Mr. Hutchison did the refereeing and the other teacher, Mr. Long helped, when he could, with evaluating and rating the different lads. There was a lot of work going on behind the scenes too as the team had no uniforms and were relying on donations and gifts with which to at least buy some shirts. Jimmy asked his dad if he could have some new football boots, which Eddie bought straightaway and he even bought a new tin of Dubbin for Jimmy to apply to his new boots. Time went by and the rumour going around the school was that a game had been arranged, in fact some sort of league had been set up or the Pelton team had been accepted into one of the existing leagues and then the team sheet went up on the notice board in the hall. All the lads rushed into the hall to see if their name was on the sheet but Jimmy just hung back, he was so excited but scared at the same time, in case his name wasn't there, so he waited and waited and finally plucked up courage to look at the sheet. IT WAS THERE, he couldn't believe it at first, had to look again and again, but sure enough there it was in the number seven position, outside right. He almost ran home from school that afternoon and couldn't wait to tell his dad when he came in from work. The day of the game dawned and it was scheduled for after school on a spring afternoon. The team changed in one of the school rooms and they were given shirts, shorts and socks to wear. The shirts were purple and pale blue and the shorts were the same pale blue and Jimmy looked a bit lost in them but he didn't care, he only wished he could lose some of the nervousness he was feeling but he figured it would go away once he got on to the field. The nervousness did not go away and he had a stinker of a game. At half-time he was dropped back to play right half 'cos he had been useless on the wing and as the game progressed he kept missing passes, letting the ball go through his legs sometimes, letting lads run past him, in fact everything that could go wrong, went wrong. The ball came to him one time, up near the touch line and one of the older lads watching said to him, "you're not having a very good game Jimmy." Of course he knew that already and he felt as though everyone was watching him and in the end he didn't even want the ball and couldn't wait until the final whistle blew. He was absolutely distraught and actually cried himself to sleep that night and being a Friday, there was no school until Monday so he had two days to try and figure out what had gone wrong and what was the matter with him. One thing he did know even at that point was that any confidence he had before the game was gone and how on earth was he going to face his team mates and the rest of the class on Monday.

On Monday at school nobody said much to him, in fact nobody said anything at all, probably suspected he was feeling bad enough but the one person he longed for to say something to him was Mr. Hutchison. Jimmy desperately wanted to be taken to one side by Mr. Hutchison and at least be asked what had been the matter. It never happened, ever. Mr. Hutchison was a young man, this was his first teaching position and it's possible that a more experienced teacher may have, at some point pointed out some things to Jimmy, maybe some guidance, maybe asked about his leg, had that been an issue? Jimmy's nervousness on the field must have been obvious, even to Mr. Hutchison who had refereed the game and certainly had other things to think about but even so. But there was nothing, and as time went on Jimmy withdrew more into himself, his classwork and keenness to learn was not affected too much but on the football field during games lesson he was not the same. The confidence was gone and there did not appear to be anyone to help and never mind the "ifs, ands or buts" but because there was no help when it was needed, it was to be years before he was able to restore his own confidence and by that time opportunities in the footballing world had long gone. Not that he was anything special, Jimmy thought years later, a legend in his own mind, as the saying goes but deep down he was hurt and eventually accepted the fact that he was only good enough to play for the house team. A week or so after that first game the team sheet went up in the hall and all the lads rushed to see if they had been picked to play in the next game and Jimmy watched and waited until he could wait no longer so he ambled casually to the back of the crowd and tried to look over the shoulders of some of the bigger kids but Jack, one of the better players, played inside left, turned and said "sorry Jimmy, you've been dropped." Those words, although not completely unexpected, sounded like a death knell to Jimmy and he just walked away, head down. He couldn't even bring himself to talk to his dad about it, he felt so ashamed, he knew he wasn't a bad player, figured he was better than one or two on the team but when the crunch came, he just couldn't perform. Was it the same nervousness or shyness that had bothered his dad, was it a family trait? He didn't know or even care at that time about those questions, he only knew that everything he had worked for, all that practice with the ball meant nothing, if you could not produce on the field.

Jimmy loved weekends, his dad would take him fishing sometimes or to a local football game or even just to a game up on the colliery field at the top of their street or sometimes down to the river, to the swings and roundabout and slide that he could still remember from what seemed years ago. Usually these outings were on a Saturday as Sundays were spent going to chapel or reading the Sunday papers or comics (as in Jimmy's case), having Sunday dinner and generally just taking it easy, getting ready for the next week. His mam, (and dad sometimes) went regularly to evening service at the Bottom Chapel as it was known, but the correct name was The Central Methodist Chapel (in 1980 the three Methodist chapels in Chester were amalgamated, Station Road and Durham Road were sold). Jimmy had been christened at the Durham Road Methodist Chapel or Top Chapel as it was known to most people, but after their move to Pelaw, the Bottom Chapel became their place of worship. Lizzie was well known at the chapel for her offers to help at weddings and funerals and other volunteer work but as time wore on and mainly because of her difficult childhood, her health was not the best, so she would miss a few Sunday evenings. But did that mean that the chapel 'do gooders' would allow her to miss her weekly monetary contribution, no sir. In fact, Jimmy, as a teenager, was in one Sunday night, his mam was very sick, his dad, Eddie, was off work, just having had a cartilage operation on his knee, Jimmy had made some ham sandwiches with a bit of Keene's mustard on his dad's and with a pot of tea on a tray had taken the tray up to them when a knock came to the front door. Jimmy opened it and it was the minister himself from the Bottom Chapel, not so much asking about the health and welfare of his mam and dad but demanding to know if the little envelopes with the appropriate amount of money inside would be continuing. Jimmy was absolutely gob smacked at the sight of the man with the collection plate envelopes clutched in his fist, each one with the date of the Sunday his mam had missed. He was about to tell the reverend to fuck right off but held back, fortunately and tried to compose himself. Meanwhile the minister was babbling on about the possibility of making arrangements for the envelopes to be taken down to the chapel by a neighbour or some volunteer when Jimmy interrupted and said, "when me mam and dad are feeling better and are well enough to attend your chapel then they will do so, when and if that happens they will decide then if their means will allow them to continue to donate, but aa'll tell yer summat, there will be no payment of back dues. Good night," and slammed the door shut. Jimmy was livid at the utter gall of the man and he was shaking a little because he found confrontations like that very uncomfortable and upsetting, especially with grown-ups when he heard his dad shouting from upstairs, "who was that at the door?" Jimmy shouted back, "nobody," and under his breath, "no bloody body at all dad."

 School life was okay but it was the weekends and summer holidays that he looked forward to. The six-week summer school vacation seemed like an eternity beforehand except that when it began, it was over in a flash but Jimmy and his mates made the most of it and the weather usually cooperated. There was a wooded area not too far away where the Cong burn meandered along on its way to Chester, finally depositing into the River Wear but the wood had been out of bounds to the lads for as long as he could remember and he never did figure out why, anyway that was the first place they went. The trees were excellent for climbing and certain tree branches just right for making bows and arrows and hand held catapults, all of which had to be secretly hidden away somewhere before going back home. There was the wood and the exploration of the pit heap, (another out of bounds place) where Jimmy and the lads had found the night-watchman's hut. The night-watchman was required apparently because the pit authorities had been informed that there were nightly excursions to the heap by people who were intent on thieving whatever coal they could find up there. Jimmy thought that you could spend all night up there and still not fill a bag with coal or anything else worth burning for that matter, plus it must be a nightmare navigating your way around in the dark, bad enough in the daylight and anyway somebody had shit in the hut so the 'watchy' was going to have to find different accommodation. Along the base of the pit heap was a drainage trench, whether man made or natural, who knew, but it stunk, it was full of all sorts of material, not the sort of material you would want to be messing around with but it did have lengths of winding gear cable, the wrapped insulation inside of which provided ideal kindling for the clay boilers that Jimmy and his mates made. The dirty trench water discharged into a stream further down and the wet clay from the stream, after the lads had dammed up a section, could be scooped up and made into an open topped box-like shape with a lid with a hole in it and the whole thing when dried out was like a miniature oven. In went the kindling, out came the matches and the boilers started blowing smoke like you wouldn't believe. When the lads got sick of this they just played football or got their bikes out, the bikes were great on the pit heap as all kinds of tracks and jumps could be made. Yes, there was lots to do in the new neighbourhood.

Early on though there were challenges for Jimmy, or did he make them into challenges? One day, he would be about seven or eight years old or so, he took out his new bike. This was a brand new lad's three wheeler which Eddie and Lizzie had saved up for and bought for him. It had bright red shiny metal mud guards and chrome handlebars and a nice seat and a bell and it was the first real bike that he had owned, other than the little toddler's bike he had in the other house and by just staying on the footpaths he could cycle all over the place without too many problems from what little traffic there was. Next door upwards lived Albert whose dad worked at Craghead colliery, he was a year older than Jimmy, next door downwards was Vic, he was about six years older and next door to him lived Paul whose dad worked at Pelaw colliery and Paul was the same age as Jimmy but was in the 'B' class at school whereas Jimmy was in the 'A' class. No significance in that, just the way it was. Paul and Jimmy were not particular friends, not in the way Jimmy considered his footballing and pit heap exploring mates friends but nonetheless there was never any bad feeling whenever they crossed paths until Jimmy had got the bike. Then something seemed to change, he sensed this change whenever he rode his bike down near Paul's house and especially when Paul was hanging around. Paul was quite a bit bigger than Jimmy and although he usually tried to avoid going in Paul's direction, this was kind of difficult considering the location of their houses and on this day, he wanted to go down past Paul's house and ride around the block. Just as in the case at school where the teachers had actually been aware of what was going on, so did Lizzie but she had not let on, she had told Eddie of course because the two of them suspected that Paul was a little backwards without being retarded, not because he didn't play with the other lads but he had occasionally demonstrated a bit of a nasty streak even with adults and his speech was not easily understood. In fact, a few years later during a gardening lesson while in the senior school Paul had objected to something a classmate had said and hurled a garden fork at him, literally skewering his foot to the ground. The teacher wasn't around to see the incident and nobody ratted on Paul because there was some sort of unwritten and unspoken code with the kids but they all had to get their stories straight and identical which they did as meanwhile, the unfortunate garden fork recipient was transported to hospital. At around the same time somebody had off-loaded an old scrap car onto the field where the lads played football. Every piece that could be removed from the wreck was removed, whether the piece was any good or not until very little was left that was recognizable as having been a car. Unfortunately the petrol tank remained and curious Paul decided he wanted to know if there was any petrol in it. What better way, he thought, than to drop a lighted match into the open neck. The explosion was heard all over the council house estate and people appeared from nowhere, or so it seemed and there was poor Paul, staggering around with a good part of his hair gone and eye lashes blown right off. "Should've blown his stupid fuckin' head off," Jimmy thought at the time. But it's not for parents of other kids to make waves and it may just have been a phase Paul was going through. It was no phase as it turned out. Jimmy was just easing past Paul's house when out sprang Paul from behind the hedge wielding quite a big stick and it appeared like he meant some mischief, Paul wasn't interested in whacking Jimmy but had decided he didn't like the bike, especially he didn't seem to like the nice bright red shiny mud guards on which he commenced to rain down blow after blow. It took Jimmy a while but then he really took exception to the damage that was being brought down on his new bike and all caution and common sense went right out of the window, in fact he lost it. He leapt at Paul and wrenched the stick right out of his hands and let him have it. Thump, thump, went the stick, Paul was desperately trying to protect himself, if his arms went across his body. Jimmy hit him on the head, if Paul's arms went across his head, the stick just smashed into his body. Jimmy was sobbing uncontrollably and then Vince's mam came out and put an end to it and Jimmy just took off with his bike, away from the house, away from everybody, just away, away as far away as he could and he never wanted to come back.

But, of course he did go back and by that time his mam knew the whole story, so did everyone else in the street apparently and it was a classic, like the joke going around the table where the final version bears no resemblance to the original version. Lizzie demanded to know from Jimmy exactly what had happened, so he told her and she had no reason to doubt his version as he very rarely told lies, just the way he had been brought up and Lizzie was very proud of the fact. She told Jimmy that some people were saying that he hit Paul with the stick for no reason when he wasn't looking and if Vic's mam hadn't come out when she did there could have been serious consequences. Jimmy just said, "look at what he did to me bike," and left it at that. The episode was eventually forgotten but Paul never bothered him again and he made a point or riding his bike up and down past Paul's house every chance he got, just to rub salt in the wounds so to speak, but he did think later on that he had taken a mighty big chance doing that. The mud guards on the bike were ruined and prevented the wheels from turning properly so Eddie splashed out and bought new ones and put them on. Same nice shiny red colour and they must have had the same magnetic qualities as the old ones had. Magnetic being that they seemed to draw attention from the worst lads on the estate. Jimmy had ventured some distance from his house, probably shouldn't have gone that far but there were new houses going up just over the bridge beside the Isolation Hospital and that meant piles of stones and sand to play on so there he was playing by himself with his bike right next him, when Fatty Clifford showed up. Jimmy knew about Fatty Clifford and had seen him around a couple of times with some other kids and as his name implied he was a chubby but strong kid with his blond hair cut in a crew cut style. Jimmy had already decided to leave and leave quickly, he knew there was trouble brewing as Fatty was ranting on about this being his area and Jimmy wasn't welcome and he was going to teach him a lesson. He could probably have out-ran Fatty but there was no way he was going to leave his bike behind so he waited to see how things were going to develop. Well, Fatty didn't hang about, he took a look at the bike and thought, "I'll have that", and he was closer to it than Jimmy was and he made a move for it. It's now or never Jimmy thought and took a swing, well it was like hitting a sack of taties[8], absolutely no effect and Fatty just used his weight to bear down on Jimmy knocking him to the ground and pinning him under his body. Jimmy wriggled free somehow and lashed out with his foot, catching Fatty right on the knee and as he was hobbling around, he kicked him again and got a punch in. Then it was wrestling time again and Jimmy knew he was beaten and was struggling to get his breath under Fatty when two men came over the bridge and pulled them apart.

"You're not from around here," said one man to Jimmy, "gerraway home,"

and the other said to Fatty, "if I ever catch you doing this sort of stuff again, I'll wallop your arse fer yer."

As he made his way home, not meeting anybody, not interested in meeting or talking to anybody, he was beginning to wonder what life was all about. Was this what the future was going to be like, fighting for yourself, fighting just to keep your own stuff from being taken from you, just because somebody else wanted it. He had withdrawn into himself a little, an ongoing trend as he was to

---

[8] taties - potatoes

discover as life progressed, especially after the episode in the school yard and he had taken refuge in his reading and drawing, he loved to draw, not very good at it but his drawings meant something to him, if not to others and these were things he could do on his own and not have to mix with others. To everybody, Jimmy was a nice little quiet lad, wouldn't say 'boo to a goose' as was the saying, and so he was for the most part but he had realised after some of those incidents that there was a darker side to him, along with a short fuse that maybe needed to be controlled. It was okay when you were a kid, all kinds of excuses were made but as you got older it was kind of different.

CHAPTER 3

Junior School Years

Life was not all fighting and proving yourself in Jimmy's world as it sometimes seemed to him. He was slowly getting his confidence back on the football field and even though Mr. Hutchison had never spoken to him directly about his poor first school football game, that was okay. Mr. Hutchison was all about producing a winning team from Pelton Junior School and if Jimmy wasn't quite good enough to be part of that team well, there were other things. He was doing quite well at those other things, his English lessons were exceptional, he was interested in History, Geography and Art and it would have been obvious to even a halfwit that with the right teacher or even just one teacher who would step outside of the envelope for once and acknowledge that maybe they may just have a pupil who was worthy of a bit more attention, then maybe Jimmy was that pupil. It has always been acknowledged that if a pupil has a good relationship with a teacher and has developed a certain comfort and trust level with that teacher then the pupil becomes more receptive to educational advice that may not have otherwise been given. That's the way it was through junior school, there were teachers with whom he got on great with and his marks reflected that and there were teachers whom he did not get on well with for one reason or another and his marks were low. Personalised individual tuition was not readily available or was not even known or even considered in 1950's North East England but there were a few teachers who would and did go beyond their boundaries to try and make a difference. Mr. Hutchison was one of those teachers who would go that little bit extra, even though he had never approached Jimmy about the school football team failure, he was the form teacher for 2A and he enjoyed being in his class and eagerly took part in games lessons where they usually just played football anyway unless it was nearing Sports Day when the class would practice different track and field events. Mr. Hutchison had brought a younger approach to all the subjects he taught and made uninteresting facts and figures, interesting. It was with a bit of sadness that Jimmy would be moving on to Form 3A where there was another lady teacher, Miss Kerr was her name.

Meanwhile Sunday School at the Bottom Methodist Chapel was playing a large part in his life and it was through the Sunday School activities that he was volunteered for the annual local eisteddfod playing a certain piano piece chosen by the eisteddfod people. Lizzie had always tried to make both Jimmy and Joan equal by providing the same opportunities for them and had purchased a used piano, a 'sit-up and beg' upright type, some years previously for Joan to practice her lessons on and when the right time came she insisted that Jimmy learn piano and go for lessons too. Well, he wasn't too thrilled about that idea, he associated piano lessons with and for sissies and the practice every day would take away all that potential play time. Nonetheless he had gone for lessons and Lizzie used to remark that he had a much lighter touch than Joan and was a better player. Yeah, right, Jimmy thought, "giving me some attaboys so I'll practice". But she made him practice one hour every day and eventually he just accepted it as part of the daily routine but on lesson day, he still refused to put his music sheets flat in the nice carrying case his mam had bought him. He would leave the house with the case and as soon as he was out of sight he would take out the sheets, roll them up as if he was carrying a newspaper, store the empty case in a hedge to be retrieved on the way back from the lesson. The eisteddfod was held in a large church hall and as he waited for his name to be called he tried to think of the piece he was going to play and the way it started. He figured if he could just get the first notes right he may be okay but the more he concentrated the less he could remember and he was getting himself in an awful state and suddenly his name was called. He was as white as a sheet and so nervous his hands were dripping with sweat as he found the way to his place at the piano and tried to settle himself, he wanted to look up and search around for someone, anyone, just a friendly face but he dared not. Soon though he realised this was his big chance to show what he was capable of and he relaxed a little and started to think clearly. He got through the piece, achieved good marks, didn't win but was congratulated by his Sunday School teachers and the eisteddfod examination panel.

His confidence was building slowly and Christmas was on the horizon when Mr. Bellson decided to put together a little Christmas Special, a nativity scene which would be performed in the chapel as part of the Sunday night Christmas service. Mr. Bellson was a regular at the chapel and he was involved to some degree with the local theatre group and had a natural flair for putting together shows of all types, he would make up the script, arrange the music if that was required, produce and direct everything and select the players. He would have some of the older members of the youth club make up stage props and although he was into musicals and plays mostly, for the younger kids it was pantomimes and funny sketches because that was what attracted the audiences. Mr. Bellson also had a delightful daughter who in turn had a delightful girl-friend and these things had not gone unnoticed by Jimmy, nor by some of his pals apparently. Mr. Bellson asked him if he would be willing to play Joseph in the nativity scene, he thought, "who has he got in mind to play Mary I wonder?" That sort of stuff shouldn't even be entering his head but he was kind of getting to like some of the girls. There had been the time when the three sisters had wrestled him down between the pews in the chapel after a service and the middle sister who fancied him was all over him and he fought as hard as he could, (well not quite 'cos she was not like Fatty Clifford or Paul) and he eventually (soon) gave up his protests and succumbed to her sloppy kisses. He thought about the experience later and had to admit to himself that he rather fancied the older sister. Anyway, Joyce was selected to play Mary in the nativity play, he liked Joyce also but she would not have anything to do with him it seemed, the rehearsals went well, there was not much speaking to do, more waving the arms and pointing to the heavens and holding the baby and trying to keep the artificial donkey and sheep from falling over. Jimmy thought at one time, "this is going to turn into a comedy", which was not at all what was intended, but in the end the play went over exceptionally well and the audience, which was the chapel congregation, loved it. Mr. Bellson had designed and arranged the props for the manger to look exactly as people would have imagined it to be, it was situated in the chapel proper between the front pews and the choir area, very basic but very effective considering the space he had to work with and Jimmy thought Joyce looked heavenly, especially reclining in the straw and he told her so but she more or less told him to bugger off.

The chapel youth club at that time was really important to young Jimmy, their meetings were held right up at the top of the old school rooms which were attached to the chapel. The building housing these rooms had been built in 1886, long before the chapel itself had been built and the rooms had been used as a chapel until 1902 when Murray's house was demolished and the new Methodist chapel built on the site of Murray's house. The youth club had a table tennis table and a room off to one side where cups of tea were made and the main room could and was used for physical exercises, practices and all sorts of discussion groups. Below, on different floors were other rooms which on Sundays were used for Bible Class studies and other classes. There was even one room which was supposed to be haunted but nobody Jimmy knew ever saw anything spooky but he was thinking that this room might prove useful for future shenanigans as nobody would go near the place. This was a good period for Jimmy, he didn't know what Methodism was, didn't even care, he only knew that he enjoyed being with the others, and it wasn't just the Sundays or the Tuesday night Christian Endeavour Group he belonged to for a while that maintained his interest, it was, just enjoyable. A new girl showed up one time at the youth club and Jimmy and she were attracted to one another immediately, they spent so much time in the tea room together that eventually they were told to pack it in or leave the club. They continued to cavort but away from the prying eyes. He even convinced her to go into the haunted room with him, "just for a dare," he told her. She knew what he was about but she went anyway. He loved table tennis, in fact he had badgered Eddie and Lizzie to buy a net and paddles so they could play at home on the dining room table, much to Lizzie's dismay. It was no-where near like playing on a full-size table but Jimmy and his dad had some great times after Sunday tea until Eddie produced the Subbuteo soccer game one birthday. This was the b-all and end-all of games for Jimmy for ever after and he watched wide eyed as his dad pulled out the end leaves of the dining room table just like for table tennis and roll out the green cloth which had the white lines for the football pitch marked on it and then proceed to install the goal posts complete with nets at each end and then position the players which were mounted on spherical plastic bases in their respective positions, "just like a real football game", Jimmy thought as his dad placed the plastic football on the center circle. When Eddie wasn't around Jimmy would play the game all by himself, taking turns for each team and he would spend hours making up team sheets and game reports as well as performing referee and linesmen duties. Better with two players he would think," but I'm getting lots of practice."

One Sunday morning, Eddie suggested to Jimmy they go fishing, it was a lovely morning and the weather forecast was good right through the day. Jimmy was over the moon, "okay get your stuff and don't forget your wellies," his dad told him. Eddie had made a couple of sandwiches and packed a flask of tea, already had the rods out and he gave Jimmy the can of worms he had pulled out of the garden earlier, to carry. They only had a couple of old rods with cheap reels and no lures but no doubt they would have just as much fun with their hooks and worms. Off they went, "we're going to go up Newbridge Bank to-day," said Eddie, "so we'll have to get a move on." A fair hike for Jimmy but he didn't mind, they took some short cuts through the houses but eventually they had to cross the main Durham to Newcastle road, which wasn't too busy as it was a Sunday and then up the bank to the bridge. "We have to get over the wall," Eddie said, "let's hope the gamey[9] doesn't catch us." This was exciting

---

[9] Gamey – Gamekeeper for the Estate

for Jimmy and a bit scary, his dad had never done anything like this with him before. "Let me get you on top of the wall," said Eddie, "and you just sit there 'til I get over the other side and help you down." They made their way down to the river, not right under the bridge but just a little-ways downstream and found a good spot to cast. They were now in the grounds of the Lambton Estate and Eddie thought it would be a piece of rotten luck to get caught considering the size of the estate and the amount of ground the gamey had to cover, but stuff happens and he would just have to talk his way out of it. This was a great opportunity for Eddie to explain a bit of the history that surrounded them and so he told Jimmy the story of the Lambton Worm and how that many, many years ago John Lambton would have actually been fishing in a spot close by and the ruins of the building they could just make out above and beside the bridge were the ruins of the old church where John should have been that Sunday morning, hundreds of years ago. Jimmy was fascinated with the story, had forgotten about the fishing and shouted, "can we go see, please can we go see." Eddie laughed at his son's excitement but said that to go see they would have to go up to the road, to the Estate entrance and through a locked gate and that would be impossible, but Eddie wondered to himself if it would be at all possible to do exactly that someday. They caught a few minnows and that was alright although Eddie knew there was good trout and perch fishing in the River Wear in places. They ate their sandwiches and drank their tea from the flask and then it was time to go home, but Jimmy couldn't take his eyes off the old ruins when they were back over the wall and on the bridge. In his own mind he was imagining John Lambton deciding not to go to church that day and then maybe wishing he had when he caught that great big worm thing on his hook. What a story to tell his mam, he couldn't wait and wanted to run home but Eddie told him to hold on a bit 'cos they would tire themselves out before they got there but inside he really enjoyed seeing his son like this and it had been a special day indeed.

One of the biggest concerns for parents on the estate up at Pelaw was not the colliery itself, as that was helping bring prosperity to the area but the fact that the railroad tracks from the pit for the engines and wagons transporting the stones and slag onto the pit heap crossed the main road. This was a reasonably busy road, not as busy as it was to become in a few years but it was the bus route up through Pelton, past the schools and on upwards as far as Consett. Beside the crossing was a hump backed bridge that allowed the traffic to cross over the tracks below, which served the coke works and other industries. There was no danger from those tracks as they were fenced off and a person had to be completely insane to venture anywhere near them, but the tracks crossing the road were a concern. There were no gates or lights, only a flag man and sometimes not even a flag man but in all the years of the pit's operation there had never been an incident of any kind. It could be argued that there had never been very much traffic and very few houses until after the war. That was about to change. What Ronny Hornsby was doing there at all, only he knows, but he went under the wheels of a rail car and lost both his legs. Ronny was a few years older than Jimmy and lived way down towards the end of the road, but his house was on he same side. A moment's distraction and a life ruined for ever. Jimmy was to see him around for years afterwards, he had one of the first motorized three-wheeler invalid vehicles available at the time and seemed able to continue to upgrade his vehicle through the years. The accident was certainly a wake-up call for everybody but as usual life went on as normal after a while. Surely it is so sad and wrong that something awful things need to happen before the message is driven home.

 As it happens Jimmy was in that area frequently, not right beside the tracks but doing gardening work at one of the pit houses. The daughter of the Deputy Manager at the pit was a friend of his sister and as her mam had passed away sometime previously they had employed a housekeeper, so he had volunteered to look after the garden at the front of the house. Not a very big garden, but it needed to be kept tidy as it bordered the main road to Pelton. He had also volunteered his gardening services at another house close by whose sole occupant, an elderly lady, was having to pay someone out of her pension money because she couldn't tackle the work herself. He sometimes demonstrated this more pleasant side which was not always evident and maybe he learned it from his mam who had always offered her services to the chapel but whatever the reasons he did not always have to be asked to 'lend a hand' and those were the sort of things that don't usually go unnoticed.

Life in the Bland house had developed into a bit of a routine by 1952, five years after the move. In September Jimmy would go into form 3A at the junior school, where Miss Kerr was the form teacher. This was also the year that he locked himself in the lavatory at home one school morning and Vic next door had to climb through the ever so small window and unlock the door from the inside. Jimmy was a little embarrassed by this affair and his friends would not let him forget it, plus he missed the bus and was late for school. How did everyone know so quickly? Being late for anything was an absolute disaster for Jimmy and this phobia was to remain with him his whole life. Maybe it was the unwanted attention it brought or being singled out in front of others that bothered him. It certainly wasn't the threat of punishment or the actual punishment, if there was any, that worried him. Even at his early age he considered it 'unmanly' to show pain or tears in front of others. On his own, though, in the privacy of his own room, there would be some emotional outpourings. He thought about his aggressive nature and confrontational streak that sometimes surfaced and wondered if it had anything to do with suppressing his emotions and should he be talking about the issue instead of immediately going on the defensive and physically retaliating. But then he would think, "if all that was taken from me with an attempt to change me, then I would not be Jimmy Bland, would I"?

Although he had friends and some were really good friends, he was getting to be known as a bit of a loner, as one relative was to remark, "he's a bit deep that one, you'll need to watch him." Whatever that meant, but it was just that sometimes, actually a lot of times, he would prefer to play for hours on his own and he enjoyed every minute of it, never even occurring to him that it may seem odd to some people. In the house he played game after game of Subbuteo on his own, playing and captaining both sides and he played ordinary Patience and Clock Patience with a pack of playing cards he found in the sideboard, this was also the place he found some of the family photographs and letters, most of which he didn't understand and was afraid to ask but he would return time and time again as he got older. He would read and read, books and comics until he was bleary eyed, then he would turn to drawing, not real drawing but more just doodling. Sometimes he didn't even mind if it was raining outside because he could do all this stuff. Then when it cleared up he would be out with the ball on his own developing his football skills.

Jimmy went missing again one beautiful sunny summer's day and it was one of those days where it was difficult to figure out what time of the day it was and nobody seemed to care anyway. Well, Jimmy didn't care, either that or the hours went by so fast for the actual time to register with him, so engrossed in his play was he. This day he had ventured into the next street and way down the bottom into the following street until he was down near the main railway. He had found, a little while ago, a small building site with the usual piles of building materials, sand especially, on a small plot of waste land and he had kept this knowledge to himself. The site belonged to a shoe maker or cobbler as he was known locally who lived around the corner from the Bland's in the cul-de-sac and business had been so good working out of his home that he had decided to build a small workshop. In fact it was a thriving business, Mr. Norman was a skilled leather worker and everyone took their shoes and belts and even their football boots to be re-studded, but nobody had any reason to think that was where Jimmy was on that particular day. Suddenly if kind of dawned on him that maybe it was time to go home, he still had no notion that it was late, well the sun was still shining wasn't it? He toddled off, not hurrying particularly at first but then he began to get a funny feeling that it may be later than he thought, the sun was still shining but seemed to have gone down quite quickly and the temperature had dropped.

Meanwhile at the Bland house, Lizzie was laying into Eddie, saying it was his fault for taking him fishing that time up Newbridge Bank and that is probably where he has gone and he should have known what Jimmy was like and she would never forgive him and the tears were flying again. Now as everyone knows, a lot of things are said that are not meant to be said and not meant to be said in that way or taken in that way when there is an incident, especially a family incident concerning a child or more importantly in the Bland s case, a second time a child had gone missing with the first occasion still fairly fresh in the parents' minds and these experiences are never, ever forgotten. But things are said and once said cannot be taken back. The neighbours were out again, chattering away, the bobby up the road had been summoned, the older lads had formed search parties and the next course of action was being discussed when Jimmy rounded the corner. John, one of the older lads, just happened to be standing on the corner and was the first to see him said, "boy, Jimmy, are you in trouble, do you know what time it is?" he looked and saw what seemed to be hundreds of people, but there were not hundreds of people of course, and he really only saw his mam and dad, surely it's not that late he thought and that was about the last thought he had for a while as Lizzie collared him and dragged him into the house through the front door which had been standing open for a long time, she was sobbing uncontrollably by that time and Eddie just left her to it but he thought, "poor little bugger." Vince next door had given Jimmy a Boy Scout pole and anybody that remembers Boy Scout poles knows that these things are pretty rigid, wooden, but with an iron rod up through the centre and they are not particularly designed for punishing kids, if they are used for that purpose with some intent, they hurt, and it did hurt, and Jimmy took a beating like he had never had before and was sent up to his room. He could hear his mam still crying and his dad trying to smooth things over but he was looking at the welts starting to come up on his legs and his bum hurt and he started to cry and he thought, "if me mam was really glad to see me like she said, how come she walloped me so hard with the stick like that?"

The original Pelton Schools opened in 1909 and consisted of only two buildings with three separately run departments each with its own Head Teacher. Because education was considered paramount there had been a series of changes even by the time Jimmy Bland was to join the school system in 1948. A new school was built in 1931 and a complete reorganisation of the schools in the Pelton area was made in 1935 with amalgamation of some and closure of others.

In 1944 the Education Act was changed to reflect the streaming of children by 'age, aptitude and ability' and secondary education, which had been introduced in the 1920's was divided into Grammar, Technical and Modern so Pelton's three age group schools became Infant, Primary and Secondary as opposed to Infant, Junior and Senior. Regulations covering the minimum number of children per class per teacher qualification had also been introduced in 1909 and this number varied from twenty to sixty and quite often teachers had more in their classes.

So going into form 3A in the junior school in September 1952 was another challenge for Jimmy as he was leaving a male form teacher and joining Miss Kerr's class. Mr. Hutchison was still the games and Physical Education Teacher so he would still have contact with him and he was getting the odd game of football now, although mostly he would find himself on the reserve list, still, he was being noticed. Moving up in the school system was not really the challenge that Jimmy made it out to be because overall he was doing fine. But school was becoming a serious affair with the following year being the Eleven Plus examination which would determine who stayed in the Pelton school system and who would go on to a different school where more advanced subjects were offered and an extra school year available to complete these studies. Passing the Eleven Plus would provide better job opportunities eventually. It is doubtful if any pupils in his age group were even thinking of future jobs at that time, in fact he knew one or two who did not consider school very important at all. As it happens Jimmy was considered a fair bet that he would be one of the few that would pass the Eleven Plus although he was not to know that information at the time.

Form 3A came and went with only the usual smattering of incidents at school, these usually ended up being punished by getting the 'stick'. Each teacher had a punishment weapon of choice, most were canes ('sticks'), and each showed the teacher's tremendous imagination and sadistic inclinations which were given free rein because the cane was deemed appropriate punishment, and don't let anyone kid you that the female staff were weaker than the male staff at dishing out the consequences for what seemed trivial offences.

There was the short bamboo stick with the black tape wrapped around one end, there was the long slender stick which bent and curved as it whistled down and lo and behold anyone who pulled their hand away as not only did the blow catch the ends of the fingers or the wrist sometimes, it also meant that the teacher experienced extra delight, almost orgasmic it has been suggested, at doing it all over again. Then there was just the normal sized bamboo cane which, over a period of time was allowed to splinter at the ends and you really knew about this one afterwards and then there was the strap, which originated with the Spanish Inquisition and had somehow got into someone's hands at Pelton. Jimmy thought that this was bad enough but was told to just wait until he got into the senior school.

 Maybe it was the thought of these various instruments of torture that contributed to an unfortunate incident about that time. One afternoon he had got involved with a group in the class who were more intent on having a good time than completing their lesson and the whole bunch were confined to the classroom for a whole hour while the rest of the class enjoyed some outdoor play time with the teacher. The unfortunate ones had been told to stay put or else. It was okay at first, telling jokes, generally carrying on without making too much noise but as time wore on Jimmy began to realise he needed to go to the bathroom, then he figured he could hold it because going to the bathroom meant he would have to go out into the school yard, summon the teacher, get permission and walk past all the other kids down to the toilets at the bottom end of the yard and then walk all the way back. The other kids in the class soon realised his predicament but what did they do? They tried to make him laugh especially when he was just standing at the back of the class trying to nip everything in the bud. Then he realised it might not just be a pee he wanted. He wanted to walk out the classroom but he couldn't, why not? Was he so scared? He was almost in tears and then in walked the teacher and at that moment he peed himself. He stood there, the pee running down his bare legs and once the flow started there was no stopping it and then there was another sensation. Oh no! The teacher was sympathetic as she told him to go on down to the toilet but she said, "Why didn't you just come out into the yard, it would have been alright". Then he had to get home, he cleaned himself up as best he could then went for the bus. On the bus it was standing room only and as he stood in the aisle, George in the seat nearest exclaimed "|Jesus Christ Jimmy Bland, have you shit yourself"? And of course the whole bus knew then and what was he going to tell his mam?

The junior school yard provided access to the senior school for the older students, otherwise their only other access was off the main road but a long way from the bus stop, so this was the short cut most senior students elected to use. A high wall separated the school garden from the junior school yard and it was down alongside this wall that the senior students walked, accessing their school yard at the bottom through a small gate. All this Jimmy had taken in but more so when it had snowed and the senior school students would band together and run like the blazes in a group down the wall towards the ever decreasing sized gate opening in the far wall at the bottom. This would happen whilst a barrage of snow balls, ice particles and other suspected missiles were hurled at them by the juniors. Jimmy made a mental note to remember this activity when or if he was to go into the seniors.

He was now beginning to get the occasional boil or abscess which would form usually on his neck, some kids get them, most do not, those things could be and often were the most painful skin eruptions ever. When he asked his mam what caused them, she told him it was some kind of blood disorder, other than that, she didn't know. What he did know was that they really hurt and took a long time to heal, but, as with other happenings Jimmy would just take them in his stride and with the help of his mam, would get rid of them. Lizzie knew the pain they caused but there was no getting around the fact they had to be bathed with very hot water and squeezed to try to get the pus out and then covered with some kind of drawing-out ointment and a bandage. With the bad ones Lizzie had to apply a hot poultice and that hurt her as much as it did Jimmy but she had to admire his fortitude, he just would not let anyone see his tears, which he kept for later, in bed when his neck just throbbed and throbbed. When Lizzie had asked the doctor one time if it was a blood problem, the doctor had said, no not necessarily, it was just one of those things.

This was the situation then as the summer of 1953 grew to a close and one momentous occasion back in June was the coronation of Queen Elizabeth and the whole street was organized with festivities of one kind or another. Trestle tables were set up and special cups and saucers were designed to celebrate the event and caterers dished out the goodies. Most of the kids had no idea what was going on but they did appreciate the feast and the extra day off school. In the September Jimmy went into form 4A of the junior school where the form teacher was Miss Lewis, a real tyrant by all accounts, and of course this was the all-important year as far as having an impact on his future schooling.

Things did not go well in his new class. Right from the start he did not like the teacher and she apparently did not like anybody, least of all little boys whom she obviously had a real distaste for. As it turned out this was the worst possible scenario for Jimmy at this stage of his schooling because he seemed to be more sensitive to a teacher's criticism than the other kids and really took exception to her name calling and ridiculing in front of the class. For all his fighting and toughness with other boys he was prone to being singled out and told he was not up to the task. In a nutshell he hated going to school when he was going to be in Miss Lewis's class for a particular lesson and it began to show especially after she walloped him so hard with the cane for some silly misunderstanding that all the good work and determination that he had put into his schooling up to that point started to drift away. He hated Miss Lewis so much that he became intimidated and even afraid of her and as the school year wore on it was quite evident that his attitude to school and schooling had changed. He got into more fights than ever before, began to get a reputation and once that happened then he became a magnet and a challenge for any kid who thought he could make a name for himself. Lizzie had noticed this change also and asked him repeatedly what the matter was but he wouldn't say until after one incredibly bad day in class he mentioned his problem with Miss Lewis. Lizzie didn't say anything except that teachers usually have good reasons for their actions and for him just to try harder, but what she did do was pay a visit to a neighbour around the corner whose daughter was in Jimmy's class, just to fish a little. Anne, the daughter said yes Miss Lewis was a bit of a tyrant and did tend to pick on certain kids and was quite adept and fond of using the cane, but what was Lizzie going to do with this information?

That last Junior School year, was a disaster for Jimmy or so he thought, he did not get one game of football for the school team, seemed to be continually in trouble and when the 'Eleven Plus' examination came around he had one of the worst boils on his neck he had ever had. This thing had three heads and was known as a carbuncle, not that he cared in the least what it was called and there was six inches of wet snow on the ground as he made his way to school the morning of the examination. Even the simple act of bending down to pick up his pencil when it had rolled off the desk brought tears to his eyes and of course the plump girl sitting at the desk next to him made a big loud issue of Jimmy's tears. Fat bugger, he thought, she'll get hers one day. The results of the examination came out and Jimmy did not pass and it was no consolation to learn that no one in the class passed but Lizzie had no doubts in her mind that a lot of the blame should fall on the teacher plus the fact that no one passed, surely signalled some sort of investigation but it never happened and school life just continued on its own merry way.

Jimmy and his mates had been eyeing the Bevin Boy huts for some time so that summer of 1954 when most of them were about to venture into the realm of senior school later that year they were looking for some adventure. The huts were arranged in an orderly fashion and had obviously been dormitories and living quarters and maybe at some time had some kitchen type facility attached. There was a brick building with a large chimney nearby, the building had probably held some heating apparatus or boiler but this area appeared to be locked up more tightly than the sleeping quarters, plus they were too close to the copper's house for their liking. Their curiosity eventually got the better of them and they drew up plans. There were only the four of them, Jacky and Tim who were in the same class but a year below Jimmy at Pelton and Bob who was the same age but went to Chester Modern school, they had all been inside the huts at some time or other and had seen the drawings and stuff and each of them was excited and scared in their own peculiar way but none of them dared show it to the others in case they lost face. Jacky was a bit of a leader and tall for his age, seemed to have no fear, Tim was tall as well but not quite as devil-may care and both were to end up serving in the police force, strange how things work out. Bob was the quiet, tough sort and Jimmy looked up to him often and Bob would eventually have a career in the fire service. So off they went to reconnoiter and find a way into the place without being seen, which they did. One side of the fenced off area bordered on their playing field so under the guise of playing football they eventually managed to create a hole in the wire fence and in they went. They weren't long inside before they realised that they were not the first to break in, what a disappointment. A broken window but no other obvious damage inside the huts which of course were completely empty. Empty of furniture maybe, but to Jimmy there was an eerie feeling about the place, men and boys had lived and slept here, not too long ago either and each one had a life and a family and a story. Had they wanted to be here? Probably not, did they consider it a prison? Possibly. Had anyone tried to escape? Would they have been shot like deserters if they had been caught trying to escape? Were there guards? Jimmy was sensitive to this sort of thing and his imagination was running rampant and then his attention was again drawn to the drawings on the walls, some were pretty crude sketches but others were brilliant art work, in colour some of them, some with personal messages attached or just the message by itself. Jimmy was imagining the beds or cots or whatever they had, all lined up along the walls and these drawings and writings would be at the head end of each one and for years that would be their only enjoyment. Working all day down the pit and maybe some nights and then back here to sleep and think and pray and draw. Nobody deserved that, he thought. Suddenly he felt like he was intruding and was brought back to the present by the lads calling to each other. They did not have time to go through each hut but made a mental note of which ones they had explored and decided not to push their luck and get out of there and afterwards they got together to share their thoughts but they all had it in their minds to try to break into the brick building next time.

CHAPTER 4

Senior School Years

The summer of 1954 was a welcome relief for Jimmy, a relief from school mostly but he now had to set his thoughts on going into the senior school in September and the thought of leaving school in another four years really filled him with dread. Eddie and Lizzie had bought him a new bike, a Hercules, sit-up-and-beg bone-shaker with a Sturmey-Archer three speed where you had to pedal backwards to change gear, but he loved it, and loved it better when he learned to control it. And those neighbours with cars loved it better when Jimmy learned to control it as there was more than one minor accident which had resulted in a bit of a confrontation between his dad and some of the neighbours. The chapel summer outing to the seaside was always a big occasion for everybody associated with the chapel, for the kids especially of course but there were parents who looked forward to the trip every year. Buses were laid on and different destinations were tried for each year and prayers were said for cooperation from the weather. Now that he was a little older he was conscious of different feelings and some of the childish pranks were being replaced by boyish tricks and comments and for, at least, that summer day all nasty things, like school, were forgotten in the excitement of getting ready in the morning, telling his mam and dad to hurry up or they will miss the bus. Lizzie and Eddie had forgotten for a while just how Jimmy could be when he was happy, "like two different people sometimes," Eddie remarked. Progress was being made with Jimmy's piano playing and he was now into stamp collecting, cars and aeroplanes, typical boy stuff hobbies. Eddie had made him a wooden garage where he could store his ever increasing collection of Dinky cars and trucks and he was forever at the library getting books out on this and that and the Sunday newspapers could not be thrown out until they were read back to front and he loved his comics with Dan Dare in the 'Eagle' and Braddock the Mosquito pilot in the 'Rover' and of course the boys' adventure books with Gimlet and Biggles. All of these pastimes meant Jimmy was spending a lot of time on his own but they were good learning pastimes and there were no complaints from his parents for this behavior. That summer the boys got together and decided to break into the Bevin Boy huts again, this time a considerably riskier venture as the brick structure was up near the copper's house so they first detoured around the far side near the pit heap, made a hole in the fence and gradually made their way through the compound until they found some sort of entry into the building. Access wasn't easy as it was obvious someone didn't want anybody in there, it never occurred to the boys that there may some danger involved, maybe some natural gas powered equipment or electrical wires or even a fall in the darkened interior. At any rate they managed to gain entry and with their flashlights switched on they looked around. The building had originally held the heating equipment and workshops but since the closure had been used as a storage for items that presumably the owners considered to be not important enough to remove at the time of closing up the place but maybe intended to come back and retrieve. The boys were all agog at their discoveries and were truly amazed to find a table tennis table, no net or paddles or balls but that would be too much to wish for. They figured there was enough room to set up the table, which they did, then they pooled their resources to see who could supply the net and such. This seemed to fall on Jimmy for some reason but he accepted the challenge and they agreed to get out of there and make arrangements to return and play.

    This was a big secret for the four of them and certainly not to be shared so within days they had the equipment together and stole back inside. There is no such thing as a quiet game of ping-pong and as the days and weeks went by and they were never discovered the boys became a little bit careless until one afternoon they heard a noise from outside and immediately froze. "Shit," Jacky said, "somebody's outside." They knew they had pushed their luck by returning day after day but the problem right now was how to get out of there, preferably without being seen. The lads hadn't been so dumb as to not search the place looking for another door to the outside, which they had found and had managed to bar it from the inside but in an emergency could get it open for escape. So while Jimmy recovered his net and paddles the others got the escape door ready and opened it slightly, whoever was out there was around the other side where they had made their first entry so they opened the door quietly and started to sneak out. The slow sneakiness very quickly changed into a mad panic dash through the huts towards the hole in the fence beside the pit heap and they could hear somebody shouting as their escape was discovered.

"Fuckin' hell," said Jacky, "It's the copper and he knows all our names."

"How's he know that", Jimmy wondered as he galloped along,

"Better spit up," somebody said although all were thinking, what's the point if he knows who they are.

That was the end of the Bevin Boy hut exploration as the bobby had visited each house and told the parents that any more of the same would result in some serious charges and names would be on record and positively trying to put the fear of God into everybody, which he certainly did in the Bland house. Jimmy was grounded and not only that but he had to fork out for a new table tennis set as he had lost everything in the escape.

Although he had been discovered breaking into the Bevin Boys compound and had paid the price, Jimmy had been excited by the chase. He told no-one what he planned to do but he stole back through the fence about a week later and made his way to the brick building. "Aa'll just have to make sure aa sees toss pot afore he sees me," thought Jimmy as he found the first entrance they had used before to get inside. It was boarded up good and proper this time, he was not surprised to see and he was not surprised either to see the other entrance boarded up just as secure." Oh well," he thought, "aa'll not hang about." But what he really wanted was to take another look at the paintings and drawings in some of the huts even though the last time he had felt like he was intruding into someone's personal world. Again he had that weird feeling that there was a presence there somewhere but he could not take his eyes off the walls, imagining the life behind each message, behind each drawing, where were they now? Were they back with their families? Were they still alive? Jimmy wished they would let this place stand forever as a kind of monument but he knew that very soon it would all be gone, and they would build more and more new houses right here on this spot.

He often got into these sad and serious moods and when he did he would go wandering off by himself, as long as it wasn't too late in the day, he reminded himself, thinking of the good hiding he got from his mam the last time. On the other side of the pit heap he knew there was a dirt road coming down from the farm which went over the railway bridge and connected with the main Newcastle road so he headed that way. He had seen a book in a shop once about railways and engines which had all sorts of numbers and names in it. It seemed like every railway engine had a name or number and it was displayed on the front somewhere. He had been so engrossed in the book that the owner had told him to buy it or scram. But he had seen some fascinating names like 'Mallard', 'Union of South Africa', 'Dominion of Canada', 'Empress of India' but he couldn't remember any more and he thought, "I bet these trains come along this line," and made up his mind right there and then to save up some money to buy the book and maybe he could check off the names one by one after he had seen them. He couldn't wait, he ran up and over the pit heap down to the farm road and continued running until he got to the bridge and he waited and waited and not one train came along and then it was time to go home. But he knew another place where he could climb the fence and sit on the embankment above the tracks and be hidden from prying eyes by some bushes. "Just wait 'til I get the book," he thought.

September came around far too soon as usual and that first morning at school after the summer holiday he felt physically sick and there was even greater apprehension this time because he was entering the senior school. But after a while things settled into a normal routine and it helped that nearly all the class from his last year at the junior school had moved on with him, so it was just a case of getting to know the new teachers and there was a new subject to be learned which was woodworking and Jimmy soon found out that he was not very good at it. He was more interested in the games teacher and the possibility of maybe doing a bit better with his footballing skills and hopefully getting picked for the school football team. Teachers tend to make allowances for new students, knowing that it is big a step going into the senior school and some kids were just completely overwhelmed by the occasion but again Jimmy's ability to read and his desire to learn, quickly made him noticeable, not a teacher's pet mind you, but he was willing to help and he was courteous and respected his elders. The first couple of months flew by and then everyone was looking forward to Christmas and the treats that the special occasion brings. It is a time for children to enjoy and no doubt some adults too until the bills come in. So then came the winter weather and the first snow fall which was quite heavy and it lay on the ground which was not always the case in north east England, quite often there was just a heavy frost but very icy and some mornings the water in the bathroom sink upstairs in the Bland house would not run away and it would usually be Jimmy who had to run downstairs, boil the kettle, run back upstairs, try to get the bathroom window open without breaking it, lean out and pour the boiling water over the sink drains which ran outside and down the wall. When this happened he had to run fast for the bus because if he missed it he was late for school. Anyway the snow was falling and it was fairly deep on the ground and he went to school but he was remembering the time when he was a junior and the senior kids ran in a group down alongside the wall and through the gate at the bottom. He waited at the top for some of the bigger lads to arrive and when there were enough of them, Jimmy tucked himself into the middle of the group for protection from the missiles and they ran. He was hard pushed to keep up and being surrounded by big kids he couldn't quite see where he was going but he figured they must be getting close to the gate opening and suddenly 'BANG', he smacked right into the wall at the left of the gate. Being one of the smallest in the group, as they approached the gate he had been pushed to the outside of the funnel and didn't stand a chance of making it through. He staggered through the opening and a couple of lads caught him before he fell, his nose was bleeding, his teeth had gone into his lip and a couple of teeth were loosened and he was almost out of it. The boys took him into one of the teacher's rooms where he was patched up and given a cup of tea. He had never, in his life had such a wallop and one of the lads said to him, "welcome to the big school, kid, we'll keep an eye on you for a while, just to make sure you're okay." Jimmy never forgot that lesson and he never forgot the two lads who had helped him. It turned out that one of the lads had already been approached by a professional football club to join as an apprentice and as he was to find out, his school and in fact the whole area was continually being scouted for local talent but what he had already noticed was the size of some of these older lads and he began thinking again of his own height and weight and if he didn't get a bit bigger he was never going to get on the football team.

Jimmy's determination and football practice had not gone unnoticed by his dad and so as a special treat Eddie decided to take him to a Newcastle United home game. Newcastle United Football Club were on a roll during that period having won the FA Cup in both the 1950-51 and 1951-52 seasons and that year (1954) were doing exceptionally well again and so every home game was a packed house. This created a bit of a problem for Eddie as they would be standing on the terraces and he would have to lift Jimmy up to see the game unless he could get behind one the steel barriers and maybe sit him on it, and this is what happened, all the fans around them helped to make sure Jimmy could see. He loved every minute of it and later when he had time to think clearly he was remembering some of the bits and pieces of conversation that were going on around him and he realised he did not understand some of the words, so he asked his dad. Eddie explained as best he could the different pronunciation of certain words depending on where the person was from. Eddie called Newcastle people 'Townies' and the word 'Geordie' was mostly applied to those who lived around the River Tyne and north of Newcastle and a sound like 'tool' was pronounced 'tooooool" in real 'Geordie' as against 'tewl' by Durhamites and a word like 'book' was pronounced 'boooooook' with an ooooh sound rather than 'bewk'. Kind of difficult for Jimmy to get his head around that but he said he understood and Eddie also explained that it was only local born people who could distinguish the nuances in the dialects and that to all intents and purposes everyone else in the world assumed that all folk from the north east of England were 'Geordies' and spoke funny and fast and all spoke the same.

It was about this time that Jimmy got another boil on his neck, not a three-headed monster like the last one but still bad enough and needed to be treated. These things just didn't disappear overnight but seemed to last forever and he couldn't fasten his shirt collar, which he didn't mind so much because he never it fastened anyway. But Tuesday night came along and Eddie and Lizzie usually went old-time dancing at Chester Ballroom so Lizzie asked Joan if she would bathe Jimmy's neck for him. Well, if Jimmy had known what was in store for him he would have buggered off right there and then, "she's like a bloody butcher," he thought as the bandage came off, and it didn't come off easy, it stuck. Joan did not seem to have the patience or the skill that his mam had and as he complained a bit of the heavy handed treatment, Joan just said, "oh shurrup you soft bugger." The torture finally ended with his neck feeling like a piece of raw meat and Joan said, "I suppose you are going to tell mam how I mistreated you." Jimmy just looked at her and thought, "you have no fuckin' idea do you?" and vowed that she would never again get the opportunity to mess with his problems.

That year also the Bevin Boy huts were demolished with the tall chimney obviously the last to go. The event brought out the whole street and Jimmy and his mates felt a little sad as another part of their history was removed, all in the name of progress.

Then Christmas was over and it was into another year and that first year in the senior school just seemed to have flown over. There were no real examinations just some small test papers in the July then it was the summer holidays again. He was twelve years old now and was with his second piano teacher, Mrs. Wilson, who lived up beside the school, which was more convenient. His first teacher, Mr Henderson, had retired and one of the few things he remembered about Mr. Henderson was his pocket book diary which had all manner of separate notes attached to the pages and the whole thing was held together with a rubber band and it looked so important and impressive and Jimmy thought, "I want to look important just like that someday". Mrs. Wilson was a lady whom he absolutely adored but his progress seemed to be minimal and Lizzie had already had discussions about changing teachers again. He had suggested to his mam that he could stop going altogether but that didn't seem to help matters. Eddie had another treat in store for him that summer and it was a trip to see an air display north of Newcastle somewhere. Jimmy was forever writing away to aircraft and car companies for photographs and drawings and so when Eddie had seen the advertisement for the air show he decided they should go. They had to get two buses to get there but eventually made it and what a show it was, the noise, the smell, the people, planes on the ground, planes in the air, planes that you could take a ride in (if you had the money), planes that you could sit in (if you lined up for an hour), planes with propellers, planes with jet engines, fighters, bombers, everything you could imagine, Jimmy had never seen anything like it, although the noise was making him feel a little sick. Then a jet plane came roaring overhead at low level, frightened the life out of him, and his dad told him later that it was an American Sabre jet and had been used in the war. Talk about being impressed, maybe that was to sit in his mind as later he joined the air cadets.

September came again and the start of another school year, this time form 2A in the senior school and things just started to take off. Mr. Walker was the form teacher and he also taught art and religious education. Jimmy liked him and very soon he was a class monitor and he learned being a class monitor was not just about dishing out paper and pencils and filling inkwells, although that was part of it, there were other perks which made him privy to some school matters. The art lesson was not taken seriously by a lot of students but Jimmy liked it and tried his best as usual and was disappointed to get a remark like 'good drawing spoilt by careless painting' in his mid-term report and his mam and dad wanted to know what that was all about. But that was it in a nutshell, he would start something, anything, a project, and then he would lose interest and it would be cast aside unfinished or just carelessly completed just to say it was completed then tossed away. Mr. Walker had seen this trend and attempted to remedy it by spending some extra time with him even though this was generally discouraged. The extra time spent paid off a little but not much and his drawing improved, not to the point that he would become any sort of artist but maybe some other type of drawing work would evolve.

His footballing had improved under the senior school games teacher and he would regularly play for the house team because there was no way Jimmy or any of his class were going to be picked for the senior school team, these were lads in their fourth and final year or possibly one kid would make the team when in his third year if he was exceptional. Jimmy had played a lot of football that summer, mostly pick-up games over in the field or sometimes on the colliery field where the lines were marked out and there were goalposts or sometimes just in the street and it seemed as if the local bobby had lost interest in chasing them and calling on the parents. This was probably because the estate had a new bobby, they were replaced every so often and some were better than others. It was during one of street games that Jimmy got into an altercation with Albert from next door. Albert was a year older and bigger, was no footballer and went to a different school and as usual with these things, nobody could remember afterwards what started the fight but a fight there was. They stood toe to toe trading blows and Jimmy was gaining the upper hand when he felt his arms being fastened to his sides, he could not believe what was happening, Albert's mother had seen the skirmish from her kitchen window, and had seen that Albert was getting the worst of it and had come out and pinioned Jimmy's arms to his body and was encouraging Albert to strike out. Which he did, blow after blow, and as Jimmy had never come up against anything like this he did not know what to do and in fact did nothing until somebody said that's enough. There were mixed emotions running through Jimmy, hurt – not so much physical, but mental and shame too and he realised he did not know how to deal with these feelings so he went home and stood in the corner of his back yard and just sobbed and that was where Tommy, another neighbour found him. Tommy had seen the back end of the fight but had come out to late to stop anything and he said to Jimmy, "come on I'll take you in the house," but Jimmy didn't want to go in the house, not just yet anyway, all he could ask was, "why, why did she do that? It's not as if I was actually hurting him, it was just a kid's fight, we do it all the time." Eventually they went into the house and Tommy explained what had happened, neither Lizzie or Eddie liked any kind of confrontations and after all, this was a neighbour who they had known for years and what was said or done at that point would probably weigh heavily on future relationships. Everybody knew that if things had just been left alone, it would have all been worked out and forgotten in next to no time, as it happens nothing was said but the incident was never forgotten especially by Jimmy.

Tommy's son Tim and Jimmy were pals, especially after the incident with Albert and Tommy began taking the two of them to Lambton Swimming Baths, down past the brickyard where Eddie worked. There was an eight until ten session on a Saturday morning and it was usually packed, this is where they both learned to swim and dive and as time went on Tommy let them go by themselves. Not only were the swimming baths close to his dad's brickyard but they were also close to Lambton pit and after the swim the two lads would go into the pit canteen and order jam butties and pop before getting the bus home. They shared a few adventures during the senior school years and it was Tommy who introduced the lads to cricket, Tim's dad owned his own proper cricket bat which he let them use occasionally and what a difference it made when it connected properly with the 'corky'[10]. Cricket was not a game or sport that appealed to Jimmy and the fact that it was never played at his school meant he did not get much exposure to it but he wasn't too bad at bat and a competent middle paced spin bowler even if the games were only with his mates

---

[10] 'corky' – Very hard cricket cork ball, rubber covered, almost always red.

on the local field. If he had passed the eleven plus and progressed on to the Grammar School then it may have been different because there they played 'The Gentleman's Game'!

The weeks were passing ever so quickly and soon the momentous event of his becoming a teenager came around, this was April 1956 and following that in September he would be going into Form 3A in the Senior School but there was the whole summer to look forward to before that happened. It was always pretty much the same crowd, Jimmy, Tim, Jackie and Bob who chummed around, not trying very hard to stay out of trouble, typical boys, so for that they were given a little leeway but when they raided Corker's orchard for the umpteen time, nobody had any sympathy when they all went down with severe belly-aches from eating green 'crab' apples and Jimmy Bland, not that he had stolen and eaten anymore than the others, but was becoming known for his weak stomach and pasty face was nearly hospitalized.

And if that wasn't enough they would occasionally raid Horner's tip which was strictly forbidden as it was near the main London to Edinburgh railway line and the tip itself was a dumping ground for all the waste material coming out of Horner's Toffee factory where Lizzie had worked for some time previously. The boys would fill their pockets with wrapped sweets but who knew why the sweets were on the dump in the first place and of course there were the rats.

Then the 'out-of-bounds' wood where the Cong burn meandered through was always full of challenges but this was the only spot where they could get the best type of wood for their catapults and bows and arrows so this was explored time and time again and one day Jimmy and Tim decided to venture there for some fun. The wood extended over the other side of the Chester road or more likely the road had been built through the wood but at a higher elevation so that there was quite a drop from the road down to the bottom where a smaller tributary of the Cong burn ran. This area was a great location for a rope swing and somebody had already attempted to fasten a rope to one of the trees up the slope. The two lads decided they would make the swing work and when it was finished they tied a weight to the end and let it go, there was no question it worked but Jimmy thought it worked too well and if you didn't get the direction just right there were a few obstacles in the way, like a couple of tree stumps, so he decided it wasn't for him. But Tim said "what the heck, I'm going to have a go". He did and he was swinging a lot farther and faster than the weight ever went but to Jimmy it was like a slow-motion dream and he could see that if Tim carried on in the direction he was going he was going to collide with one of the stumps. He was shouting a warning, Tim saw the danger and was trying to manoeuvre but he just started spinning slowly, and then he crashed into the stump with his back taking the full force. Tim screamed in pain and Jimmy flew down the slope and behind him ran two men who had been doing some repair work on the road. At first they all thought Tim had broken his back as he was sobbing uncontrollably but after some tender investigation from the men they figured there were no broken bones, only some very bad bruising so they helped carry Tim up to the road and along to the steps leading back up to Pelaw. It took the pair of them a long time to gather their wits and get some colour back in their faces because they were scared, scared of what had happened and scared of what might of happened and what story were they going to tell or if they were going to tell anybody at all.

Ironically, that year Eddie and Lizzie decided to make their annual summer holiday a trip to Blackpool, taking Jimmy with them as they always did. The six year difference in ages between him and Joan meant that the two of them never seemed to go on holiday together. Blackpool was a favourite spot for lots of holiday makers, lovely beach, great fairground with the well known big dipper called 'The Grand National' and of course Blackpool Tower. As a special treat for him they took him to the 'Derby Baths' one day, this swimming pool was Olympic size and there was a special show starring Johnny Weissmuller, otherwise known as Tarzan and Jimmy had seen all the Tarzan movies up to that day and just loved his exploits with Jane and Cheetah. Well, he was over the moon especially when his dad bought a programme and right in the middle was a glossy photo of his hero complete with loincloth and huge knife. They waited for what seemed an eternity as some other swimming and diving events took place and then there he was. He appeared huge to Jimmy and Weissmuller was a big man but Jimmy wasn't sure it was Tarzan because he was not wearing his trade-mark loincloth or knife, he was wearing a swimming costume just like his dad's and he said as much to his dad and then he said, "where is going to swing from"? Eddie had to chose his words carefully so as not to totally disillusion his son but eventually succeeded but then all Jimmy could think of was Tim flying through the air on their home-made rope swing and crashing into the tree stump. "Did Tarzan ever do that"? he wondered, but he never mentioned any of that to his dad.

The rest of the summer was uneventful, the usual fights over marbles, cigarette cards and petty squabbles that developed into fights over nothing and Jimmy had no problem finding things to do on his own if stuff like that was happening but somebody organizing a game of football would bring him out of his shell. Then suddenly it was September again and the thought of school just made him feel sick to his stomach but it had to be dealt with and what made it worse was the continuation of excellent weather, feeling like it is the middle of summer is not the sort of time to be going back to school. Not long after the start of the new school year, on a brilliant sunny Saturday Jimmy and Tim planned to meet after lunch, they had already been to the early morning session at Lambton Swimming Baths and had had their jam butties and they had decided to try out their home-made darts. The darts were made with four matchsticks bound together with some home-made glue with a pin protruding from one end and hand-made paper flights inserted into the other. The balance and flight of these things was phenomenal and they had made fixed targets where points could be scored depending on where the darts stuck. But that wasn't enough, they had to get more adventurous and began throwing them in each other's general direction, Jimmy was behind the parked car, Tim was at the other end of the car, Jimmy peered over the roof of the car and the dart was suddenly in his eye, just like that. Left eye, automatic reaction, hand comes up, knocks the dart away, he came out from behind the car and says, "it went in my eye." Nothing immediate but Jimmy knew the dart had gone into the white part of the eye and that was the end of that game. It was a shock and he kept hoping that maybe it didn't go quite in the eye but he knew deep down that it had and even though he could not feel anything at that point, he suspected that it just would not go away.

    Jimmy went home feeling awful, not from any pain but more than a little scared. He kept looking in the mirror for signs but could not actually see anything different but he was already beginning to feel different. Now maybe that was just the worry of what had happened, he thought, so he went to get ready for his piano lesson which was later that afternoon. Lizzie was out shopping, Eddie was at the Newcastle home game, he had nobody to confide in, was that a good or a bad thing? The piano lesson was in Chester, with Mr. Armitage his new teacher and went off alright, with not much waiting around for his turn which was not usually the case and Jimmy came straight home. "What's wrong with your eye?" Lizzie asked him. "Feels like I've got summat in it," he replied. Lizzie wanted to take a look at it but Jimmy shooed her away and said he was going to lie down, which was not like him for any night, let alone a Saturday night, Lizzie thought. Eddie and Lizzie were going out dancing that night and Jimmy just lay on the couch, every hour that went by his headache got worse until he just up and went to bed. He slept on and off, actually praying that in the morning everything would be fine but it wasn't and all through Sunday right into the evening he just lay on the couch and the headache got worse. Lizzie was very concerned now but did not know what the problem was and Eddie was not much help because he didn't know either and Monday morning came, Eddie went to work, early as usual, Lizzie just took one look at Jimmy and wrote a note out for the school which she took around to Anne's because Anne was in Jimmy's class. Anne suddenly blurted out that she knew what was wrong with Jimmy and explained what had happened on the Saturday. Lizzie was horrified so she rushed down to the doctor's surgery in Chester with Jimmy in tow. Being Monday morning there were quite a few waiting but Lizzie pushed ahead and the doctor took one look and told her to go immediately to the Eye Hospital in Newcastle.

    Lizzie was desperate, Jimmy was close to tears, she was asking him why on earth had he not said what had happened, surely it was not something to be quiet about or be ashamed of. They got to the hospital and after a brief initial look at the eye an emergency was declared. Jimmy was in the emergency room and on the operating table within the hour and people in white were asking him to lie still while they inserted some sort of clip into the eye to keep it open. He was absolutely petrified and almost peeing himself and he felt so cold. Meanwhile Lizzie was speaking to the doctor and he said and confirmed later that another twenty-four hour delay would have not only seen Jimmy lose his eye but his life as the poison was just coursing through his system and in those early hours they were still unsure of the outcome and of course Jimmy was admitted. Talk about shell shock, Lizzie went home in a daze, asked later, she could not remember getting home from Newcastle.

Those first couple of nights in the hospital were a bit hazy for Jimmy, when he tried to remember later, he just knew his head throbbed, right behind the eye and his backside was like a pin cushion from all the penicillin injections. Daytime was bad enough but at least there were things going on in the ward that took his attention away from his problems. It was a large ward, quite a lot of beds down both sides and one or two beds on each side of the door at either end. His bed was immediately to the right as you came through the top door and next to Jimmy was an older gentleman who was in for a cataract operation, his eye condition had been brought on and made worse by brushing into a rose bush while gardening at home. Jimmy took a real liking to the man and it was during one of those early nights when Jimmy was having a particularly tough time, the pain was almost unbearable and constant and he must have been moaning out loud because the night nurse came and told him to be quiet as he was waking up the other patients. Well the older gentleman just laid into the night nurse and told her to leave him alone, couldn't she see that he was in pain and why not give him something. It had some effect because the nurse came back a little later and had Jimmy take something. His eye was completely covered, in fact the bandage covered half his head and to pass some of the time during the day he tried focusing the other eye on the clock on the wall opposite above the other door. "Yeah, not bad", he thought, "I can see that quite clearly", and then he started to look around at the other patients, most were older men, well, everyone was older to Jimmy at that stage. He never knew what progress was being made with his eye, if any, only knew that his backside was more sore than it had ever been because of the continuing injections and the headaches had not really gone away. It was during one of his morning look around that he saw a group of medical staff gather around the bed of the patient right opposite Jimmy at the other end of the ward. They maneuvered the little table so that the doctor could reach whatever was on it and Jimmy was horrified to see that it was a huge syringe and with one person on either side of the gentleman holding his head perfectly still, the needle was inserted into the back of his eye. he was sweating profusely by this time and didn't want to look but couldn't take his eye off the proceedings." Jesus Christ" he thought," please do not let that happen to me".

The next morning they were there, at Jimmy's bed, early, before he had even time to think about the day ahead. The old man, his friend, in the bed next to him thought to himself that those frequent penicillin injections must not have been having the desired effect because the eye injection, as far as he knew, was used sparingly, all he could do was watch and pray. Jimmy didn't think he could move even if he wanted to, he was literally frozen to the spot with fear. The doctor was saying something but it may as well have been Double Dutch as far as Jimmy was concerned, the syringe was there, he felt something, not exactly pain but something uncomfortable and then it was done and the bandages were being re-applied. The medical team left and he just lay there, not moving for what seemed hours until he heard the old man saying something, asking how he was feeling. Jimmy struggled to try and figure out just how he was feeling and then he said, "I'm scared, so scared," and the old man took hold of his hand, gripped it firmly and said, "hang in there son, you'll be ok." Jimmy turned away as his tears started to flow.

The next day the old man, his friend, was gone, maybe he had told him he was going to be discharged and he had forgotten but he missed him straight away. There were visitors for Jimmy at night but there was only one hour of regular visiting and there were restrictions on the numbers of visitors, still he looked forward to the visits, whether it be family or friends, but the days were long and soon he had a new neighbour in the bed next to him. A younger man this time who did not seem to have the same friendliness as his older gentleman friend, but they got on alright. After the eye injection there were some signs of improvement, there were less backside injections now and the headaches were becoming easier to handle. What was worrying Jimmy now was that the clock on the far wall was starting to look a bit blurry as he looked through his good eye, the bandages remaining in place over his bad eye. He would blink furiously and wipe with a cloth but it didn't alter his vision, so he mentioned it to the doctor one day and the doctor had explained that it may not be permanent, it's probably a bit of eye strain caused by the covering up of the other one for so long. Jimmy was not so sure.

What he was sure about was that people generally spoke different around here, not a different language but as he had been exposed to nearly all Newcastle born people lately there were some words that were said with a different sound than what he was used to. He tried to remember the conversation he had had with his dad after the football match. In fact, what Jimmy was hearing was true broad Geordie in some cases and a lot of it was barely understandable depending on where the person was from. Most people, as they get older and move into different areas and get jobs, tend to tone down their native dialect a little especially when going for interviews but in the mining villages and shipyards up and down the Tyne people didn't move from job to job, their whole lives were spent in the same place and there was no reason to change how they spoke, in fact it was the locals themselves who could not understand out of area visitors. Even though Jimmy had been born in Newcastle, his whole life to that point had been spent in County Durham where there was a noticeable difference in sounding some words. These differences were only noticeable to locals, to anybody else everybody talked funny and they were all 'Geordies' whatever that meant.

Three weeks went by and it was time for Jimmy to leave the hospital but there was to follow weeks and months of outpatient visits and the eye was to remain covered for a long while yet. This period of missed school and missed opportunities did not appear to affect him too much but obviously his footballing dreams had taken a bit of a bashing just when his confidence was beginning to build up to a new level, not a great deal to do about it he thought sometimes, just keep on trying but it was a difficult time for him and he was ever so glad to get be able to remove the eye patch but still had to where dark glasses especially during the winter weeks of 1956/1957 when there happened to be snow and bright sunshine. He never did like to draw attention to himself but wearing those glasses did exactly that and he tried leaving them off once or twice but got headaches so bad he decided just to deal with attention. When it was time for the school Christmas meal and dance he immediately decided not to go but then after consideration and some considerable persuasion from his parents he relented and ended up having a good time. He was without a partner for the first time ever as Alan had absconded with his usual girl, Ann, during his time in the hospital, good friends will do that for you, look after your girl-friend while you are away but nonetheless he ventured into the school hall with the eye patch in place and thought, "this should do the trick", and sure enough there was one girl who did not have a partner and she eyeballed him straightaway. She wasn't in his school class but he didn't mind that because he was looking at her good sized boobs and he began praying for all the dances to be slow ones and as they were about the same height there was no danger of getting his other eye poked out. He had a great time and was to meet with the young lady a few times after that.

The school year came to a close in the July and he dealt with whatever tests the school laid out for him and his class and when July came around and he left for the summer holidays he was without the dark glasses and seemed a bit more cheerful about his future, because he had to be thinking that one final year at school and he would no longer be a schoolboy but his mam and dad had a surprise in store when they told him they had made arrangements to go on holiday to Wales and they had booked a caravan. This was certainly different and as Jimmy had only seen pictures of caravans, his imagination was running away with him and all Eddie had to show was a simple picture, but it looked great. Wales is some distance to travel and quite a transport challenge with luggage and tickets and transfers to different buses and it wasn't until long afterwards that Jimmy appreciated just what they had achieved. After everything they had all gone through recently as a family this was going to be a dream holiday and they were all so excited, the only problem was Jimmy starting to get another boil, on his nose this time. What caused these things to develop? Excitement? Stress? What? No option but to grin and bear it because there was no way he was going to miss this holiday.

The holiday was a complete wash-out. The caravan stunk of disuse, there were earwigs in the drawers, the field where the caravan was parked was ankle deep in water and it rained and rained. It rained so much that the roads were flooded and they almost missed the night out at the circus because they could not get across the intersection to get the bus until some gentleman came along in a big truck and ferried them across. Absolute disaster made even worse because of the boil on his nose which decided it wasn't going to go away anytime soon.

CHAPTER 5

Final Senior School Year

The disappointment of the washed-out caravan holiday in Wales was not forgotten for a long time and even though parents cannot be held accountable for the weather Eddie and Lizzie felt bad for their son but they would never admit that was the reason they bought him a second-hand bicycle, a Dawes Emblem with Derailleur gears and he could not believe his good fortune at having a mam and dad as good as those two. He thought that he should make a better effort to do more in the house for them. Jimmy and his dad rode the bus to Sacriston, about three miles away and then they walked back with the bike. To Jimmy it was a racing bike but it was classed as a road bike, it had dropped handlebars and a racing type seat, which was not very comfortable but that didn't matter a hoot and a dynamo for lights at the front and the back and it was red. It was not one of those fancy lightweight jobs but with some care it would last a while. Better last a while thought Eddie because we won't be buying him another and when Jimmy said he wanted to take off the mud-guards to make it look more like a racing bike, his dad absolutely refused to have anything to do with the idea, saying it would spoil the look of the bike, not to mention the mud and stuff being flung up and onto his back and backside. He immediately joined a cycling club just outside of Chester and used the bike to get to the YMCA which he had joined a year or two back to upgrade his table tennis skills. He had been playing table tennis regularly at the chapel youth club and thought he was a good player, bought himself a Slazenger bat and figured he could make a good account of himself amongst his own age group. There were quite a few chapel club members at the Bottom Chapel, both old and new, young and old, Jimmy was always hankering after one of the girls and was considering asking one for a date when one night it was announced that a table tennis tournament had been arranged in the next town and the competition would be against chapel youth clubs and non-chapel clubs. This brought great excitement and a flurry of training and practice sessions were arranged as the competition was the following week. The day of the competition dawned and they all took the regular bus to the town and the venue was very well organized with numerous tables set up and officials and overseers all raring to go. After all the registrations were complete the tournament got underway and it was all singles matches. The way it worked, each player played a set of three games, the match winner was whoever won two out of the three games, then both winner and loser refereed other games.

Jimmy had a hard time, he was experiencing the same nervousness he had had years ago in his first junior school football game, playing in front of an audience of friends and strangers. It wasn't that he didn't play well, he just could not win and time was passing so quickly and the more he tried, the dread of not winning a game became more of an issue. The time flew by and then the tournament was over, refreshments were dished out after the tables had been cleared and trestle tables were set up and everybody was laughing and joking and having a great time seated at the tables. The announcement of the winners came over the loudspeaker system and there was lots of cheering and good natured booing. Then he realized that the organizer was going through each game listing the winner and the loser and making some well-meaning comments and Jimmy thought, surely not, he is not going to mention my name and the fact that I never won a game, but he did, and there were hoots of derision and name calling and he felt as small as an ant, and he vowed never, ever, to play anything in public again, he felt he did not have whatever it takes to handle that kind of situation. "Here we go again," he thought. He knew that these were the kind of incidents that brought out that other side of him and if anybody said anything, even in jest, he would go straight on the defensive and would want to strike out, to say something nasty without even thinking, not even meaning what he was saying and even to start throwing punches. It had happened so many times before.

Jimmy was happy just to on get on his bike and ride, ride anywhere, but on his own and the competition was himself and he would race and set himself times and push himself to the limit but he knew that was not what he really wanted, he wanted to play on a team, play a sport, be good at it, not just average at everything which he seemed to be and he also knew that he could not let his other side loose whatever the reason if he was to keep his reputation as an okay lad. That was the situation going into the final year of his schooling, he had been told that there was some sort of examination at the end of the school year, the results of which may point in a certain direction for his future but that was a while yet. In September he went into Form 4A of the senior school and he had been noticing for some time that his sight was not as clear as it should be and just as soon as he noticed it, he tried to dismiss it but it really began to bother him that year as he had joined the Air Cadets. Jimmy had never been one for the Cubs or Boy Scouts in fact, he had gone to a Cubs or Scouts initiation/new members' meeting a couple of years previously and was not impressed, he thought at the time that half of the current Boy Scout members would have been better off in the Girl Guides. He had persevered though with his attempts to join something and had ended up in the Boys' Brigade where he spent two highly forgettable years, but he had learned some outdoor skills like camping and trying to get a fire going in a thunderstorm and eating cold, uncooked baked beans straight out of the can and lying awake the whole fuckin' night because he was wringing wet. It happened that when he made up his mind to leave the Boys' Brigade, a few of the other lads had also decided to leave, well that pissed the Captain right off as he took it personally so he called them into his office one at a time to question their reasons for departing such a wonderful organization. Jimmy's reason was the only one acceptable as far as the Captain was concerned and this was to join another organization which happened to be the Air Cadets. So here he was in the Cadets on the rifle range trying to see the target, he tried changing hands, well that was like a right handed person trying to play a left handed guitar, no wonder his score was zero as was pointed out when the targets were collected, "lucky nobody got shot", Jimmy thought. It wasn't only the firing range but there was Aircraft Recognition to be learned and it would have been a help if some fuselage details could be made out or even the shape of the plane could be a little clearer, he certainly could not apply for a post as an anti-aircraft gunner so it was quite plain to see that something had to be done. What brought the situation to a head was the day the eye doctor visited the school. One by one the students were called into the cloakroom where an eye chart had been set up and a mark had been placed on the floor at the appropriated distance from it. Jimmy's turn came and the procedure was to cover one eye, read the chart then cover the other eye and read the chart. He covered his right eye first, this being the one that got the dart a year or so back, that wasn't too bad, not excellent but passable and then he covered the left eye. "Go ahead," said the nurse, "read the top letter and then continue downwards." Jimmy could barely see the chart, never mind the top letter, he could not believe how bad his eye sight had become. Obviously the strain on the good eye caused by the cover up of the bad eye for so long had cause permanent damage but his brain had been sending a message to his eyes to compensate for the difference in eye strengths. Bugger, he thought, I'd going to have to wear glasses like a sissy.

But a sissy he certainly was not and this was highlighted by his efforts when he went to camp each summer with the Air Cadets or Air Training Corps (ATC) as it is officially known. The previous year, had been his first camp and these camps were intended to give the cadets a taste of life as a serviceman on a real, working air base. There was an initiating rite for new recruits on camp and this took place at the first opportunity on the arriving Saturday. Jimmy had heard about the 'ceremony' but thought no more about it as the first few hours were taken up with going to the stores and picking up bedding and cutlery, finding the billet that had been allocated, learning how to make a 'bed-pack' properly, as this was inspected every morning and had to be made again and again if the corners were not square and dimensions were not right, then generally learning the do's and don'ts and rules of the base. There was time for a bit of relaxation in the billet when all that was done and then Jimmy was aware of a quietness that had not been there before when he noticed a couple of junior NCO's heading towards him and his pal Bob. Jimmy just up and ran and although he made a good account of himself there was physically nowhere to run and eventually he was caught and dumped on his back on the floor and suddenly his pants and shorts were yanked down around his knees and his balls were covered with black boot polish as a tremendous roar of approval erupted. But Bob was a different story, rather than succumb to the embarrassment he decided to go out of the window, forgetting he was in a second story billet. So now things were a little more serious as the NCO's tried to grab hold of Bob any which way they could as he hung onto the window ledge for dear life. The incident did not put an end to the initiation rite as maybe it should have because it reared its ugly head again the following year although Jimmy was not a new recruit that time and he was a year older and on the Sunday night after arriving he managed to down a few pints at a local pub and got well pissed. How he managed to get the beer, nobody knew but he made a complete fool of himself. He was severely reprimanded and physically punished the following morning before being allowed to rejoin his squadron but the lesson was learned. The remainder of the week saw him knuckling down to assignments and duties and doing his utmost to erase and have his squadron mates forget just what a disgrace he had been to himself and to them.

For years now, Eddie's work had been treating the employees and their families to a Christmas pantomime, usually at Sunderland Empire. Jimmy loved these outings as each year there would be some well-known person playing a part, somebody he had seen on television or at the pictures and there was always a part for the audience to play, "behind you," was the popular cry from the kids as the villain tried to sneak up on the unsuspecting victim. When the opportunity came to play a part in the chapel Christmas pantomime he jumped at the chance. Dick Whittington was the name of this one and as Mr.

Bellson wrote all the pantomime scripts he sometimes changed the characters and the story a little because in this one Mrs. Whittington was in it and Jimmy played a small part where he had to address her by name. Well, he must have had some sort of mental block on the night of the pantomime 'cos no matter how hard he tried he could not remember her name, there was a deathly silence and Jimmy just stood there like a tin of milk then he blurted out, "Mrs. Whittaker." Well, George, who was dressed up as Mrs. Whittington, just burst out laughing and so did the audience but Jimmy went bright red and just wanted to disappear. Finally everybody agreed it was good for the show, pity it was a one night only performance.

For some years when Jimmy got the chance he would go to the Saturday afternoon matinee at the Palace in Chester, this place was nicknamed 'The Lop House' by all the kids for probably obvious reasons. It cost about six pence and they usually showed cartoons first, then trailers for up-coming movies, then a 'B' picture which was usually a western and then the main picture which was often 'Flash Gordon' or somebody like that. It was great entertainment for the price, but even at that price there were some who would attempt to get in for free. Everybody knew there was a way in through a small side window which led to the toilets but it wasn't every Saturday that attempts were made until one particular Saturday Jimmy had decided to go and he arrived early to get in the line. There was a bit of a commotion going on around the side of the building where the toilet window was located and it seemed like somebody had got stuck half way through the window. Two lads managed to pull the unfortunate kid out and he tumbled to the ground like a roly-poly pudding Jimmy thought and then he looked again and sure enough it was Fatty Clifford. Jimmy should have kept his mouth shut, he knew that but he said, "ya shoulda known better then to try and get yer fat arse through that window Fatty." Clifford struggled to his feet and retorted, "you again Blandy, ah'll finish off what aa started," and took a run at Jimmy but he was ready for him and stepped to one side as he smacked Fatty around the side of the head catching him off balance. Seizing the opportunity, Jimmy got in a couple of good punches but despite Fatty's girth he was no slouch and size does matter in some cases as he caught Jimmy smack in the mouth. Just then the manager of the picture house came out with another chap and separated the scrappers telling the two of them that they were barred for life from the Palace Theatre and he would remember their faces so not to try and come back.

"Will aa never learn to keep me mouth shut," Jimmy said to himself as he made his way home, his mouth was sore but he didn't think any more about it until next morning, and being Sunday he was kind of looking forward to catching up on a few things, although he did have Sunday School in the afternoon and then he realized he had also committed to going to the Sunday morning service. This had been an agreement with his mam as she wanted him to start going to evening services with the adults. He had washed his face and was about to brush his teeth when he saw the face in the mirror had a gap in the two front teeth, "like a bloody goalpost," he exclaimed. "Now what am I to do"? he thought, "can I leave it like this? Actually doesn't look too bad but I'm not going to get too many girls looking like this, bugger it, I'll leave it for now and see how things go." So that was how it was going into the Christmas holiday period, the last Christmas holiday at school, made him feel a little bit down and a little scared because he still had no idea what he was going to do with his life. He liked to draw, not artsy fartsy stuff he would tell people, but proper drawings with a tee square and a set square and measuring lines and angles and his art teacher had encouraged him in that respect although there was not much Technical Drawing taught at the school, still, maybe that could be followed up. Even though it was the school holiday season, Sunday chapel services just never stopped, whatever the occasion, so Jimmy and his three mates who, over the years had formed a special friendship and had certainly been through a few escapades together, met at about nine thirty on the Sunday morning and entered the chapel. They had been given certain privileges in return for providing services like helping some of the older members to their seats, making sure the hymn books were dished out and taking the collection plates around so a pew nearer to the front had been allocated just for them and this worked out alright because the morning service did not get jam packed with people like the evening service. Of course they had been made to put on their Sunday best clothes, suit and tie with a white shirt and shoes polished, together with matching socks and as they sat there they looked like tailors' dummies out of a shop window thought Jimmy. As the service and the minister droned on, there were a couple of hymns, the reading of the lesson for that day, messages to be read out, death notices, marriage banns, if any, and then a bit of a lull before the sermon. There was a bit of a buzz of conversation, but not loud because most people felt like the chapel was not the place to natter and hang out the dirty laundry, although that would come later. It was this quiet period in the service when one of the lads farted and anybody who has sat on one of those wooden chapel or church pews knows that if there is no attempt to nip the sensation in the bud then the sound would be like a clap of rolling thunder and it was. The lads looked at each other and there was no way that Jimmy was going to be able to hold in his laugh, he was nearly peeing himself trying to keep it together and show some restraint and decorum. They all just managed to hold it in but every so often during the sermon there was a muffled titter which nearly set them off again. No doubt they would be spoken to so as soon as the final Amen was put forth so immediately the chance came they were off, running out the side door and there was such a roar of laughter as all that had been held in check was let loose and the really funny part of it all was nobody owned up, nobody ever knew who the culprit was. Of course, one person did.

Jimmy was looking forward to Christmas as all kids do (or should) but he was older now and not really into little boy toys but one thing the Bland family had always encouraged and made happen was playing games and usually a Sunday night was set aside for just that, whether it be a simple game of cards or a board game, even Snakes and Ladders, the old stand-by. Lizzie did not like to be shut out every Sunday night while her husband and son played Subbuteo, which they would play all night if she let them, so she put her foot down and insisted that they play something where they could all join in. But books were still Jimmy's favourite, and he was always at the library; he had read 'Treasure Island' by Robert Louis Stephenson umpteen times and seen the movie, and had read over and over that other classic 'The Coral Island' by R.M. Ballantyne and even at school he had enjoyed the class reading of 'The Thirty Nine Steps' by John Buchan. While searching around old book stores and markets in Newcastle for stamps for his stamp collection he had stumbled across 'The Saint' books by Leslie Charteris and they just fascinated him, especially the older ones which were set in the pre-World War Two era and he would search for hours on end for issues that he had not read and ended up with quite a collection. Much later when the 'Saint' television series started he couldn't wait to watch it but then was so disappointed as the script writers had totally misrepresented the character, changing him from a partly reformed gangster still with ties to the underworld, who robbed the rich to feed his own lifestyle to some kind of debonair, smooth talking choirboy type absolutely perfectly played by Roger Moore but completely wrong. The books he really did prefer were the Football Annuals that his dad bought him because not only did they have write-ups of games but action drawings of his heroes. For some time, Jimmy and three of his school classmates had been thinking of forming a band, Jimmy was a member of the school choir although he secretly thought he had been selected because he could read music and would be able to turn the pages for the pianist at the appropriate time. He had obtained a guitar with a carrying case and Billy, the obvious leader and most musically talented of the group, ("the only talented member of the group", had been a comment from the Headmaster)), had shown him how to finger a couple of chords. Not really learning guitar music theory but at least Jimmy knew about notes and chords from the piano but a piano could not be carried from gig to gig could it? So over the Christmas holiday period they got together and practiced a little. The years around 1957 were the beginnings of rock and roll which as a form of music was still frowned upon in certain parts but 'skiffle', now that was good old clean stuff and relatively easy to play. As a group they played whatever tune was dominating the hit parade at the time as long as it wasn't too hard to learn or to play. For a couple of years they played at local youth clubs and school dances and actually had a place to practice which was above a store not far from the school until it came out that the owner of the store was into little boys, not that any of them really understood the issue at the time or what 'into little boys' meant but the parents did and the other thing that the parents objected to, especially Jimmy's mam, was the time they got a gig playing Sunday lunchtime at a local Working Men's club where beer was served and she clearly demonstrated her refusal to let Jimmy go anywhere near the place.

But football was the love of his life, probably because he had more of a natural ability with the ball than with other things and he never considered practice a chore to get around or avoid altogether which was the case with other activities including playing piano or especially playing piano. The problem was he just never seemed good enough for a team or there always seemed to be someone better at his position, and as time went by and he didn't get to play, his confidence took a hammering, this, usually at times when he needed a bit of a lift. It was during one of these more somber moods, February 1958 it was and February of any year is enough to make anyone somber, he had just finished his newspaper round and was running a bit late for his tea at five o'clock because the family were all sitting around the kitchen table about to start their meal when he walked in the back door. The atmosphere seemed kind of quiet, more so than usual he thought, when Joan broke the silence with, "have you heard the new.". "No," he said, "what news?" Joan continued, "The Manchester United football team have all been killed in a plane crash." The silence this time was overwhelming, Eddie could hardly look up from his plate and muttered something like, "it's terrible, all those young boys," as Joan went babbling on but Jimmy was not even listening by this time, as he noticed the evening paper on the table with headlines blazing. Eventually news started filtering through and it was all bad, eight of the United team had died and the list was there, "no, not Duncan Edwards as well," he said mostly to himself as he thought back to just a few nights previous where he had watched young Duncan Edwards on the telly playing for England and it wasn't only Jimmy who thought that this lad was the very future of English football. An absolute disaster and as hindsight is the greatest thing since slice bread, everybody agreed that the plane should not have taken off under the icy conditions especially since it had already attempted to get off the ground once. Debates would rage for years but there was no question the football world had lost some greats.

Even though Lizzie and her son had different priorities regarding the importance of the piano she was ever so pleased with her decision to change his piano teacher a couple of years previously, even though this came with an added cost for Mr. Armitage was well known and respected in Chester's music circles. He was very much involved with the local operatic society and provided numerous musical scores for their shows. He also arranged Royal Conservatory of Music examinations for students who warranted them and as Jimmy had shown ability and promise whilst taking the Grade One examination the previous year, he had been put forward for the second examination which was to take place before the end of his final school year. There was lots happening in Jimmy's life, he had had a couple of road races with the cycling club, didn't achieve anything except experience but what he did like about the club was that they had a football team and he was part of it. The team belonged to a makeshift league with half a dozen other teams and they had got permission to use a pitch belonging to somebody else, so, other than looking like a rag-tag bunch sometimes, they gave it a go every week and Jimmy loved it. The things that had helped maintain his fitness level was his involvement at the chapel youth club, where they had football skills training in the large concert hall, his cycling to the YMCA at least once a week and he had got into the routine of running home from school every night, which was about a mile. Until one afternoon he left school as usual after the bell went and started his run. The route was pretty much wide open, it was the same road the bus took and there was only one house about two hundred yards from the school then there was nothing for three quarters of the way home until the farm was reached along with a few houses and a pub. This solitary house was set back from the road quite some distance and it was reached by a dirt road with hedging on either side and there was always a dog sitting outside the front door of the house which barked at everything and everybody but was securely chained up, so Jimmy as usual just ignored it. He had just reached the dirt road leading up to the house when he detected a change in the tone of the barking, "holy shit," he said out loud, "the fuckin' thing's loose." And loose it was, it was coming down the dirt road as fast as its legs could move. He turned around and in one movement was running as he had never run before, he could see that the bus was in and probably waiting for the last students to arrive but it seemed an awfully long way away and the dog was gaining and slavering all over the place, probably with the thought of sinking its teeth into fresh meat. He figured it was going to be a close thing but he was beginning to gasp a bit and knew he could not keep up the pace but the thought of that dog's teeth ripping into him spurred him on. The bus was getting closer and he could make out the driver and conductor looking in his direction but what could they do? He was just yards from safety when the dog clamped its smelly teeth onto his leg, he was wearing long trousers but that didn't matter, he didn't stop running and reached the bus with the dog still clamped to his leg, he threw his school bag to the bus conductor and then kicked out at this animal fastened to his leg, it loosened its grip and by this time there were people at the bus stop who managed to chase the dog away. Jimmy was as white as a ghost and shaking like a leaf which was generally his state in difficult times like this but the bus conductor got him a seat and returned his school bag and slowly his breathing returned to normal but that experience was to last a lifetime and would forever affect his attitude and feeling towards dogs.

The dog attack happened on a Thursday and he hated Thursdays because of the huge amount of weekly periodicals and radio and tv guides which made such a heavy load for his paper route but that particular week seemed to have been full of incidents. On the Tuesday, he was on his way home after finishing his newspaper deliveries and had just reached the top of the steps which led up to Pelaw from the Pelton Fell road and was taking a bit of a breather. He saw, across the other side of the field, a man walking his dog, it was a small terrier type dog and was on a long leash because there was no one else around, when out of no-where appeared a large German Shepherd dog. This animal made straight for the smaller dog and grasped it around the throat with its powerful jaws and just would not let go despite the man's efforts to shake it off. He was kicking it, hitting it with a walking stick and screaming and sobbing uncontrollably at the same time but it made no difference. The small dog's struggles became weaker and weaker until Jimmy could no longer watch and his own tears were falling as he got on his bike and slowly rode away. "What could I do, what should I have done?" he thought many times afterwards and those two incidents, happening in the same week destroyed most affection he would normally have had for pets, dogs in particular.

Jimmy's time at school had been well spent, especially the last four years and the topic of failing the eleven plus often came up but with no real closure on the subject, after all what are you going to about it now? But over-all he had done very well, had worked hard, received good marks and generally had been amongst the top students in the class, so it was no surprise he was being lined up for the position of Head Prefect which was an honour indeed. It was around this period, shortly after the Christmas holidays of the last school year that Albert, next door, who was a pupil at Chester Modern School, showed Jimmy a joke. It was written on two sheets of paper and Albert said to copy them and let him have the originals back straight away, which Jimmy did because he thought at the time it was a good joke and worth the effort. The two pages each represented a letter and a gift to a girlfriend. One gift was a pair of girls' panties, the other gift was a pair of gloves. The two gifts and consequently the letters got mixed up and reversed and the rest was left to the imagination of the reader. The following day Jimmy took the joke to school and during the morning's break between lessons, waiting for the teacher, he handed it out, so it was being passed from desk to desk in a secretive way or so they thought. Kids tend to forget that adults, including teachers, were kids themselves once, hard to believe sometimes but it is a fact, and the teacher for that lesson, who just happened to be the games teacher, suddenly made an appearance. Well, everyone knows the feeling,

"what's going on?' asked the teacher.

"Nothing,", was the chorus of innocent replies.

When it is plainly obvious that something is going on and poor Mel who had been left holding the parcel as in the game, 'passing the parcel', where if you are the one caught in possession of the parcel when the music stops you have to pay a forfeit.

"What have you got there Mel?"

"Nothing sir."

Jimmy thought, this was not how it was supposed to be and knew there would be repercussions of some sort.

"Let me see,"

so out from under the desk came the two sheets of paper grasped in Mel's hand. The teacher took one look at the contents, obviously got the gist of it and said,

"where did you get this?"

Then the question went from desk to desk until it came back to Jimmy.

"And where did you get it, Bland?"

"Got it from a lad who goes to Chester Modern sir."

"So you are responsible for it?"

And when that sentence is said like that, it is not a question and a simple, "yes," was the response.

The consequences of being discovered as the owner of the joke resulted in a caning of six of the best on the backside over the Headmaster's desk after the humiliation of being called out of gym class and in the Headmaster's study he was also told to forget about being Head Prefect and think very seriously about the possibility of being expelled.

For four years Jimmy had been top or near the top of the class in every subject, he had run errands for the Headmaster, he had been entrusted with privileged information, he had played sports, he had been a class monitor each year, he was a member of the school choir and now he was being threatened with expulsion and not only that but the Headmaster was threatening to tell his mam, this, Jimmy pleaded with him not to do and he never much pleaded with anyone. The outcome of all this only reinforced his opinion of the hypocrisy of authority and it also reminded him of the story of the 'Greek Tycoon':

'One day the Greek Tycoon was standing with his pal on the hilltop overlooking the harbour and what a vista it was. The brilliant sun shining down on the beautiful blue/green water where all manner of craft were moored and going about their business. Around the harbour were buildings, old and new, together with the hustle and bustle and colours of the market place with the stalls and vendors trying to entice customers, a truly wonderful panorama. The Tycoon said to his pal, "do you see the splendid harbour down there? I built that, but nobody knows or remembers. Do you see the new hotel just over there with its swimming pools and tennis courts? I built that but nobody knows or remembers. Do you see the beautiful casino also? I built that, but nobody knows or remembers. Look at the cruise ship just getting ready to sail, I built that, but nobody knows or remembers. Even the market place, I rejuvenated all that, but nobody knows or remembers. But you fuck one goat"............................

The few months leading up to July seemed to be full of tests and evaluation exercises at school, all geared up to try and determine where the students could be best placed in the work force. A group of employment experts visited the class one time and went around each desk individually asking what the student wanted to be. Can you imagine such a dumb question being asked that bunch? In reality it was a really good idea but it was a shock to the system for the majority of Jimmy's class to be even thinking of working for a living. Did we have such a good time at school that we did not want to leave? Probably not so much a good time but a time to be remembered, mostly for good experiences, certainly they were all new experiences and without a doubt, school years would be looked back on more than any other singular event in most peoples' lives. It is probably the imminent threat of responsibility which is to be landed on our shoulders that is the worrying factor and heaven forbid that we start wishing we had done this and not that even before leaving school for the last time.

Jimmy had not needed to be told that the end of his schooling was fast approaching and for some time had been writing to various companies for information on employment, in fact this was a continuation of him writing to places asking for photographs and specifications for motor cars, aeroplanes and even military vehicles, really just kid's stuff but he had amassed quite a dossier of useful information although he would be the first to admit that not every reply was a potential job opening and what job would he be actually applying for? It was becoming more and more evident that he was best suited in some sort of engineering draughting environment, he could not draw pretty pictures or people to save his life but had a modest understanding of some engineering principles and had seen how some engineering drawings were presented. One reply from an electrical engineering company grabbed his attention, not a job offer as such but this particular company specified they would be hiring apprentices in the near future and if he was interested then he was to write to them and they would add his name to the list of candidates for consideration. Jimmy really did not know anything about engineering practice especially the electrical side of it but the company was relatively local, located just outside Newcastle and apparently they had put out the advertisement well in advance of their requirements to enable them to pursue a thorough vetting procedure which consisted of a preliminary written examination and on successful completion of the examination the candidate would then design and build a model of some sort and then attend an interview with his model for assessment. He was overwhelmed by the requirements of the tasks ahead if he was contacted and doubts about his ability to even compete at this level were just running rampant through his head. In a big way he was flattered and proud to be in the position of actually applying for a job like this but deep down he knew he just did not have what it would take to win through and there were not too many people who could really help him, it was his confidence or lack of it that was nagging away at his guts. His mam and dad were so proud of him and would think no less of him whatever the outcome but could only offer well-meant advice to the tune of, "do your best, that's all you can do," and that was it in a nutshell wasn't it? If a person can look back on their life and say they had done their best, what more can be asked of them?

  The letter came one day, asking him to attend the company's premises for the purpose of writing an examination, mixed emotions

A NOT QUITE A GEORDIE STORY

again, amazed to have been selected, scared to death of taking an examination where he would be made to look a fool, doubts assailed him and he even thought to stop the whole thing right there and then and he would have no worries. Jimmy had never been one to shirk any challenge so he figured what the heck, he'd come this far and if he didn't go through with it he would forever wonder. The day came and not knowing just what form the examination would take he had not been able to prepare in advance so he gave himself enough time to get there, changed buses in Newcastle, asked the bus conductor to let him know when the stop came and presented himself at the company's reception desk. The examination was held in a large assembly hall with more than ample room between desks and there were dozens of applicants, of all shapes and sizes and up until that point the company's representatives had gone out their way to make everyone welcome and to try and calm those nerves, Jimmy's nerves were not calmed by any stretch of the imagination. As usual with examinations there was a time limit and everyone got stuck in and nerves were forgotten, Jimmy's problem was always time, or lack of it, he either did not grasp meanings immediately which meant re-reading the question or he just simply had mental blockages because he allowed nerves to get the better of him. Anyway the bell sounded for time and it was a relief just to be able to walk out of the place and make his way home.

Life quietly resumed on its regular way, at school a Head Prefect was named, Jimmy thought that Andrew Mackay was probably a good choice. Andrew was a studious type, didn't play sports at all, seemed sometimes to be too perfect in his manner, especially with the teachers, "but that's okay," mused Jimmy. Andrew's big hobby was photography and he was easily persuaded to tell anyone who showed the slightest interest, about it. Jimmy was a little interested in the subject, didn't know anything about it of course, but during a conversation, Andrew suggested he come up to his house sometime and take a look at his workshop and he would give him some tips on how to get started. They made the necessary arrangements and Jimmy showed up at his door one Saturday morning. Andrew was an only child and his dad must have given him just about anything he wanted as he had his own dark room, two or three cameras, good ones as well, enlarging equipment, proper lighting for different settings and other stuff about which Jimmy had no clue and Andrew went on and on describing the photographic process as if he were in front of an audience. Jimmy had to admit that Andrew knew what he was about but was quickly becoming bored but his interest perked up a bit when Andrew started talking about getting him going if he was really interested and Jimmy thought maybe he was going to be given a camera, or something special like that, wouldn't that be great? Andrew reached up to where some photographs and negatives were drying on a line above them and took down a peg, one of a number that were not being used and handed it to Jimmy, "there, that will get you started," he said. Jimmy just stood there, trying to digest what had just happened and not knowing exactly what to say. So he said," that is wonderful Andrew, are you sure you can spare it?" with just a hint of sarcasm. He would have burst out laughing but the whole episode had been so serious and he really was disappointed, he just wanted to get out of that place as quickly as possible but Andrew continued babbling on as if he had demonstrated some momentous act of charity. Jimmy made it to the front door and then he was outside, realized he still grasped the little peg and threw it into the hedge and for once he was speechless and just shook his head in disbelief. Needless to say, photography as a hobby played no further part in his life.

Jimmy improved his cycling with a close finish in a road race and made a point of showing up for the Saturday morning football matches, his chapel table tennis tournament fiasco was almost forgotten and he had glasses that he was supposed to wear for distance which he absolutely refused to do. He had managed to save a little money from the evening newspaper round that he had had up until recently but he had run afoul of the shop owner after failing to deliver his last call of the day one Thursday. He hated Thursdays with a passion because this was the day all the weekly magazines came out which had to be carried and delivered along with the evening paper and he would have difficulty riding his bike with the additional load. Well, on this particular Thursday it was pouring with rain, a non-stop downpour and he had the longest route of all the kids, one end of the town to the other so even with his cape on he was just soaked and freezing cold. He delivered the second-off last lot then looked at how far out of his way he would have to go in comparison to the direction of his house, he thought bugger it and threw the whole bundle in the closest hedge. Of course the consequences of his actions had to be faced the next night when he went into the shop to sort out his evening newspapers where the owner collared him before he even started his sorting. "Mrs. So and So didn't get her papers and periodicals last night and she particularly likes her 'Womens' Own' and 'Radio Times', if you couldn't deliver them you should have brought them back to the shop," he was yelling. Jimmy started yelling back figuring he wasn't going to be called out in front of the other kids like that so he shouted, "I have the longest fuckin'route and I don't get one extra penny from you, you miserly bastard and in any case the shop was closed by the time I was finished so I threw her bundle in the hedge." That was the end of Jimmy's newspaper delivery career especially when the owner shouted, "you're fired," and the reply he got was, "stick your shop up your arse." The worst part of it all was he lost a week's wages and now the only money that he had was the pocket money given to him each week by Lizzie but he managed to save a little and for what little he saved Lizzie would give him an equal amount if it was to buy something useful like clothes as he was becoming aware of styles and fashions and the fashion for some young men was the Edwardian or 'Teddy Boy' look which basically was a jacket of extra length and drainpipe trousers. This mode of dress was not to every adult's acceptance for along with the distasteful appearance (to some) there seemed to go an open disregard for authority, any kind of authority. The weeks drifted by, the weather was warmer with the forecast promising a nice summer ahead, end of term school examinations were complete but results in Jimmy's class were not up to expectations especially mathematics for the boys and those wonderful teachers put their heads together and came up with the bright idea of making the boys sit the mathematics examination over again and to help them achieve better marks, all game's lessons including football, along with woodworking classes were cancelled and in their place extra mathematical study was enforced. Jimmy didn't mind missing the woodworking classes because he had never achieved much success with that subject but even so he would rather have woodworking than mathematics any day and he imagined the teachers huddled together in their common room giving themselves 'attaboys' for coming up with such a brilliant idea and making a note to try it again the following year.

The letter arrived from the electrical company where Jimmy had completed the written examination, he just let it lie there unopened on the table where his mam had put it. Eddie came in from work, Joan was already in from her job, Lizzie put out the evening meal and there was the usual small talk about the day's events, the meal was finished, the dishes were cleared away and Joan suddenly said, "well aren't you going to open it then?" He wanted to open it later in the privacy of his own room but he knew that was out of the question now, so he slowly slit open the envelope and pulled out the single sheet of paper and read it to himself. They knew, they knew by the beaming smile on his face that he had passed the examination, no details, just that James Bland had been successful in passing the entrance examination and would he please follow the instructions in the letter. Well, everybody was hugging him, his dad was shaking his hand and Jimmy just stood there, overcome by the occasion and not knowing whether to laugh or cry but already was thinking ahead to the next part which was the making of a model and the interview.

He never knew who it was because he could not remember telling a soul about the letter or the examination but one morning, at school, in the main hall at the general assembly, when the whole school was still in attendance, the Headmaster made an announcement which pretty much detailed Jimmy's success in passing the entrance examination for a job at a prestigious company and that all that remained was for Jimmy to complete the interview. He was horrified by the announcement which not only singled him out in front of the whole school but now increased the pressure on him to be successful in the interview which he knew was far from the case. Jimmy thought, "it's all about making the school look good isn't it? Fuckin' teachers haven't a clue about how to deal with kids and their feelings." Having resolved the mathematics problem to the acceptance of the powers that be, the school lessons were now almost back to the normal routine but even the teachers were not too bothered about the classes as long as everybody behaved and the noise level was kept down so Jimmy was able to work at his woodworking bench uninterrupted and the first thing he had to do was to decide what to make to take to the interview. The best thing he had made to date in woodworking class was a small foot stool which he had constructed out of hardwood, stained and varnished it and with some neat decorative chisel work had made it look quite a worthwhile project. He had taken it home and after the initial 'oohs' and 'aahs' and isn't that nice, it had ended up in the rubbish because one of the legs fell off. Probably best to make something small so it can be carried easily thought Jimmy but making something small usually meant being extra careful with details and he was not a carpenter or cabinet maker by any means. He decided to make a cigarette box and set about drawing up the plans which he completed without too much delay. The company had not allowed a great deal of time to complete the task and he knew he would need every minute of it to actually make the box so his plans were not the best to look at but they at least were workable. While the rest of the class just seemed to idly pass the time, he labored furiously onwards, there was help and advice available from the woodworking teacher but obviously no hands-on assistance. The time flew by as he knew it would and he could not get the dovetail joints right and the box was not exactly square and the lid did not fit properly and as panic set in the problems with his project increased. The date of the interview was fast approaching and he was almost finished but it really was a botched-up job and he knew it and in a fit of exasperation he decided he was not going to take it, as in his mind it was awful, so into the rubbish bin it went.

There was an outer room where the applicants waited their turn to be called and as Jimmy looked around at the models they were holding, he was amazed and more than a little envious. There were metal worked projects, wood projects, actual working models of engines and home-made gadgets of remarkable design ingenuity then he looked down at his empty hands and sweaty palms. One by one they were called in and one by they came out until Jimmy's name was called and in he went. It was a boardroom with one of those huge oval tables in the center of the room with about a dozen suits sitting around it, immediately very intimidating. The first question was obviously regarding the model, or lack of a model, as this had been a significant request and part of the assessment. Jimmy's explanation was that he did not have time to finish it so predictably the follow up question from one of the suits was, "why did you not bring the plans with you?" "Sorry sir, I never thought to bring them," Jimmy stammered. There was much scribbling of pens on paper, and he thought later that that particularly stupid decision of his to toss the plans away could have made a huge difference to the outcome of the interview as the plans were really quite presentable. He could kick himself sometimes for his impetuosity. The next few questions were not bad and concerned his hobbies and his involvement with sports and club memberships and he was pretty much at ease with his answers and his confidence was growing then,

"do you know what an alternator is?" followed by,

"what is a transformer then?"

He knew right there and then he was finished and done like dinner, he knew he was applying for a job at an electrical company, why on earth had he not spent some time looking up electrical terms instead of playing Subbuteo or reading comics? Another suit asked him if knew what a capacitor was or a resistor, as far as Jimmy was concerned they could have been items found in an Italian food store. Then a glimmer of hope – a suit that had been sitting quietly scribbling asked," in the electrical world, what do the terms ac and dc refer to?" Jimmy had read something about this, thinking about an electrical train set he had seen in a store, he was sure it was something about a dc controller being required for the operation of this train set, but he could not find the words for an intelligent answer so he mumbled something about model railways. The suits finally decided to give him an easy one, "do you know how to mend a fuse?" Well Jimmy knew the answer was not to insert a piece of cigarette packet foil between the terminals or to explain that his dad fixed all the fuses in the house or that he had never had any cause or reason to even look at a fuse box so he meekly, almost whispered, "no sir". Lots more scribbling of pencils on paper and, "thank you for attending Mr. Bland, we will be in touch, good luck." Jimmy walked out of there emotionally just spent, he made it home in a complete daze, not even remembering the journey when he thought back later. His confidence was at the lowest level it had been for ages and he did his usual trick, retreated into himself, he would hardly talk to anyone and when his mam and dad enquired about the interview, he told them to forget the whole thing.

He was now into the remaining two or three weeks before the end of term and also the end of his school life as he reminded himself. He still kept to himself most of the time, hardly confiding in anybody, had dropped out of the YMCA, but was planning to go to camp again with the Air Cadets in the summer, that would take his mind off things a bit he thought, especially as this camp was going to be under canvas and not billeted in regular servicemen's quarters, on a large working air base. He had persevered and accepted his eye-glasses as being necessary and now had no worries going on the rifle range which he would be required to do at camp and he wanted to do well because competitions of one kind or another were always arranged between visiting squadrons of cadets. He had already received a letter some time ago from the electrical company confirming his worst fears just stating that unfortunately his application for apprenticeship had not been successful, no surprise there he thought, when, at school one day, right out of the blue, he was called into the Headmaster's study, he immediately thought, "shit, what have I done now?" but the Headmaster seemed to be in an agreeable mood and no mention at all was made of previous misdemeanors and transgressions. Mr. Anderton, the head, did ask about his interview and Jimmy just made light of it saying he was not successful and was a little intimidated by the whole thing and just left it at that. Mr. Anderton said he was sorry to learn of the outcome, (Jimmy got the impression he already knew) but the head went on to say that he wished to discuss a proposal which Jimmy may find interesting and it would at least require some serious thought. Apparently a college in the North East of England had been selected as one of the venues for a new type of drawing course being introduced in the United Kingdom. A limited number of places, probably twelve, would be available at each selected college, so the selection of students was extremely important as was the selection of schools which were to supply the students. The name of the course was 'Technical Illustration' and at the completion of the course students would be expected to take a 'City and Guilds of London Institute' examination. Mr. Anderton did not know anything about the course contents, nor was he expected to know but Jimmy appreciated the faith and trust that the Headmaster was placing in him and he was overwhelmed with emotional feelings at being selected by the Headmaster after some of the bone-headed things he had done and he just stood there for a moment with his mouth open, not knowing what to say. The Headmaster was saying Jimmy needed to discuss all this with his parents as it meant a year or two at college with all the expenses attending college involved but an answer or approval was required very soon so as to get things moving, and he was just standing there in a daze but eventually he came down to earth and thanked the Headmaster very much and walked out of the study. Talk about emotional turmoil, his head was in a whirl because usually being summoned to the Headmaster's study meant trouble and this was a complete reversal and was there no one he could talk to? It still comes down to the question, 'do teachers really understand the enormity of situations and decisions being placed on children? Do they expect an adult response from a child who cannot possibly know the futuristic results from a wrong decision? He was over the moon at being selected to go to college and do whatever this important new type of course meant and Eddie and Lizzie never even thought twice about giving their approval and so at the end of the school year in July 1958 Jimmy Bland left school.

CHAPTER 6

Art College

As it turned out, he wasn't leaving school, not just yet anyway, more like going from one school to another but the two schools were totally different as he was to find out very quickly. There was a summer to be negotiated first, between the beginning of July when he left the senior secondary school and mid-September when he was enrolled at Sunderland Art College. It never, for a minute occurred to Jimmy to try to estimate the cost and sacrifices his mam and dad were making to make it possible for him to go to college, this sort of thing kind of dawns on people later on in life when they are in the position as parents making a decision for their children, then reality sets in and lights come on. This is where that magic word 'hindsight' earns its reputation. Often mentioned in joking fashion as in, "hindsight's 20-20 isn't it?" or even just, "hindsight's great isn't it?" How many people find themselves looking back sometimes thinking, "if only I had made a different decision then," or "why did I not do that when I had the chance?" Some decisions are made for you or you may not be in a position to make an assessment, all kinds of factors and circumstances are involved but nonetheless there are occasions when we have full control of the situation and have all the information necessary to make the correct decision and these are the rueful ones to ponder later in life. Jimmy often went back in his memory to the 'eleven plus' days where success in that examination would have changed forever his future, but then the other side of the coin is he would not have been given the opportunity to enroll in a new, country-wide drawing course. The biggest difference and positive note in passing the 'eleven plus' was the opportunity to go to school at least one extra year, possibly two years and the exposure to the stepped up subjects that are available to students and then possibly going on to university.

Anyway life is what it is and whether Eddie was trying to get a message across without making Jimmy feel guilty, which is doubtful, but he had suggested a fill-in job at the Brickyard may be available for the summer weeks if he was alright with the idea, but first they had a summer holiday planned. "Don't worry", his dad told him, "It's not another caravan" and he laughed as he saw the look on the lad's face. Jimmy had thought about the Post Office as a sorter or a telegram boy but if truth were known he probably would still be thinking about it when September came around so this opportunity was not to be missed and he agreed to go to the Brickyard. The holiday was indeed a surprise and two weeks later they were off to Butlin's Holiday Camp in Ayr, Scotland and even if it rained they had their own chalet and lots of indoor entertainment to choose from and if it was nice and sunny the beach was right there. Butlin's Holiday Camps were very popular and they were scattered all over the United Kingdom, the first one having been introduced by Billy Butlin years earlier before the Second World War and the one at Ayr was originally a Training Camp built by the Ministry of Defence during the war which Butlin reclaimed at war's end. The entertainment was first class, organized and hosted by 'The Redcoats', a team of professionals, many of whom were to become household names in the stage and television industry after plying their trade and gaining valuable experience at the various camps. The highlight of the week for Jimmy was not one of the amazing shows that he had seen but watching the antics of four young campers, all coal miners from around the Chester area and their paths crossed at least once per day because they were designated the same dining area and meal times. They were funny and they were fun and they danced and sang the nights away but some mornings as the week wore on they looked the worse for wear but they never failed to make a lot of Jimmy every time they met. Eddie and Lizzie knew the four young men were drinking a fair bit at night and sometimes they would hear them before they saw them singing 'Alexander's Rag Time Band' which was an old hit made popular again at the time. Eddie was a little concerned that his son may pick up some of the words that were let slip and other comments because he was at such an impressionable age but he didn't interfere too much. And then it was time to come home.

Back home there was a party to go to. Living in the streets around Jimmy there were a number of kids who had gone through the same school system, some even in the same class for year after year and who had become special friends, even the parents had become friends over the years but this one girl in particular, Linda was her name, was special, the pair of them had really grown up together but had not spent a lot of time with each other, they just knew they could visit each other's house and it would be fine and it would be just one of those relationships that would last forever regardless of the other's circumstances but there would never be any romantic attachment, was that was a mistake, who knows? Linda had an older brother about the same age as his sister Joan and Jimmy just admired him, the way he dressed, the way he spoke, he seemed rough and tough but was always laughing and joking and Jimmy adored just everything about him. Probably every boy has this hero worship at some point in his growing up stage so it's a normal thing as long as it stays a normal thing. Linda's fifteenth birthday party was coming up at the end of July and Jimmy was invited. He kind of hoped that maybe Linda would be unattached but there she was, at fifteen already going out with someone and the boyfriend was there, obviously, and never left her side but it was a good night with some good games that Jimmy had no idea existed especially the ones that took him into a private room in the company of a girl who seemed to know a lot more than he did about 'things'. The best time he had was with the girlfriend of a boy who lived just across the street from Linda and that experience was a real eye opener, more than that actually, but at the end of the night everybody just parted company as if it had been the most normal party in the world and probably it had been, but not for Jimmy. The only thing he could really remember afterwards about that night was that girl's lips on his lips and Bobby Darin singing 'Dream Lover' which was played over and over again and which was to remain his favourite song of all time. It was because of Linda and her boyfriend that Jimmy continued his cycling club activities as they were all members of the same cycling club and without them he no doubt would probably have lost interest sooner than he did and he had done some good riding in his short time there so he again needed another influence to pressure him to continue with his interests. A recurring theme, because of his preference to be alone and his awkwardness in the presence of others he continually needed to be encouraged and coaxed to get out of his shell and be convinced that he was okay, normal, the problem was that there was not going to be someone always available to keep motivating him.

He thought the world of Linda, not to the point of being obsessed or paranoid over the issue but he had no way of expressing his feelings because it was obvious that Linda had no other eyes than for her boyfriend and there were times especially when they were all together cycling to the club for a meeting or whatever that he felt like just saying something, just to get things out into the open but he could not as he knew that would destroy all relationships. Why should he spoil other people's relationships because he could not get one of his own? All he knew was that Linda had been a part of his life for many years and without realizing, they had formed a lifelong attachment but the type of attachment that Jimmy wanted or thought that he wanted was not and never would be in Linda's mind. He decided he had better knuckle down to some serious thinking and the first thing was to prepare himself for work at the Brickyard. His job would be to help load lorries with new bricks for delivery to various building sites or stacking bricks in the yard or just general clean-up duties in the yard and for this he would be paid five pounds per week with a Saturday morning option for an additional pound per week. The hours were seven am to five pm with half an hour for lunch and he would need to kit himself out with suitable working gear. Eddie had told him it was hot and dusty and showed him how to make protective pads for his hands as the bricks could either be hot or rough and sometimes both. These protective pads were fashioned from the rubber inner tubes from lorry tires and were slotted in such a way that the fingers could slide in leaving a full palm covering and for the thumb there would be a separate piece. Eddie was worried because he had noticed a boil forming on Jimmy's forearm, it would be the last boil he would ever have and it would be the first one on a place that was not his neck or his nose but the brick dust blowing about would make it difficult for the boil to heal. He had a new 'bait'[11] box and felt ten feet tall at the thought of going to work, his dad had said they would not be able to travel together because Eddie's job required him to be there at least half an hour before the shift started but that didn't matter as Jimmy was just looking forward to doing this whole thing on his own, but obviously knowing that his dad would be around just in case. His dad had made a point of mentioning that the Brickyard was probably the worst place to work if you had a boil, whether it be on the neck, arm or anywhere else and Jimmy just shrugged off the concern but secretly it was hurting pretty bad and he thought that if he could just keep the bandage intact it would be okay and of course Lizzie was tut-tutting and saying he needn't go if he didn't want to. Well, that made him more determined to go and he vowed he would not let anybody go soft on him but it's hard to hide a bandage on an arm wearing a short-sleeved shirt or a tee-shirt and not attract comments but these hard guys were concerned individuals at heart so there were times when it was obvious that Jimmy was in a little distress so they suggested he go with the lorry driver on his delivery to the site and just help unload and then come back. It was the same when he was asked to go in on a Saturday morning. His work would be different on the Saturday and would be to go on to the top of the kilns together with two or three other lads (men) and make sure that each kiln had an ample supply of coal for fuel for the burning of the bricks in the sealed kilns below. The firing of the kilns was a seven day a week, twenty-four hours a day operation, the operators were called 'firemen' and Eddie had been a 'fireman' in his earlier days at the yard, so keeping the kilns supplied with fuel was a very important job. The top of the kilns' roof, from a

---

[11] Bait - lunch

distance, was flat but in reality there was a cross-work of six inch or eight inch raised structural walls. The coal was dumped in one area of the roof and had to wheel-barrowed to each kiln loading port which meant negotiating the raised cross-work walls. This was achieved very 'scientifically' by installing eight inch wide wooden planks so the wheelbarrows could be run up and over the walls. Jimmy had watched his dad work the special wheelbarrow he had, going into the newly opened red hot kilns and loading the wheelbarrow with sixty red hot bricks and coming out and returning time after time until the kiln was empty and even in the winter months wearing just trousers and singlet and he looked at the wheelbarrow he had been allocated for transporting the coal and although it was just a regular shaped wheelbarrow it looked awfully heavy especially with a load of coal in it. He watched the other lads do it and of course they made it look easy so he thought, "well here goes." No problem along the flat portion of the roof and then up onto the plank, need to be going at some speed he had been told, he got almost to the top of the wall and lost it, his arms and wrists struggled to hold the wheelbarrow on course and he just had to let it go, it toppled over, dumping its load of coal all over the place. He felt awful but the lads said, "divn't worry, it's nowt, try again with less coal in the barra." It was a tough slog for an extra quid a week but he managed and he also earned the respect of his fellow workers which was worth more than any amount of money to him because he knew that some sort of report would be drifting back to his dad and the last thing he wished for was to let his dad down. Jimmy enjoyed working with most of the lads although there were one or two that didn't hesitate to give him a hard time, maybe because his dad had got him a job there, who knows, but he wanted to be like them, to be accepted by them and he found himself slipping into their rough way of talking and was remembering that time in the hospital when he had been scorned for his pronunciation of certain words and the difference between being a 'proper Geordie' and not being a real 'Geordie'. Well, here in the Brickyard, everybody kind of spoke the same and as far as Jimmy could remember it was not 'proper Geordie' but he was learning to identify the different accents and dialects from the Durham and Sunderland areas and nobody ever told him he talked funny. But his mam was concerned and told him so, she said, "just because you are working with those lads does not mean you have to speak like them or act like some of them. You don't hear your dad talking like that". And of course she was right, as always.

The summer weeks sped by and Jimmy took a week off work to go to camp with the air cadets, for the most part he enjoyed those weeks away, sometimes he had a problem with the discipline which was over-enforced at times he thought and he struggled in certain competitions which seemed to favour the bigger and stronger lads but overall the training was good for him and thoughts had crossed his mind that maybe there was a future for him in the armed forces. Another piano examination was taken and passed and he was becoming quite a gifted player but he still needed sheet music in front of him to get through any kind of musical piece. He probably was not practicing enough because there seemed to be so much going on at that point in his life that he felt he needed to neglect something and it turned out to be the piano, much to his mam's dismay. He knew people who could listen to a tune and then sit down and play it but it was never going to be the case for Jimmy Bland. The highlight of the summer for him was, as it had been for years, the chapel trip to the seaside but something happened which caught him quite off guard. He realized he had a crush on one of the girls and this was a girl who lived close by and was one of his group who had been going to the youth club for years, to afternoon Sunday School with him and for the last little while had been going to the chapel evening services with him. He could not figure why this crush had just miraculously manifested itself but it had and it had been quite evident coming home from the last Sunday evening service, where, instead of appearing nonchalant and casually modeling his new blue suit with the silver fleck and red jacket lining complete with new thick soled shoes commonly called 'brothel creepers', he was reduced to a babbling buffoon in front of her and his pals. Not having had a crush before, nor would he have another like it, he was at a loss to know what to do or say and ended up being just embarrassingly red faced and silent. Later that night he realized that she had been in his thoughts off and on for a while but only now when he thought about her, she appeared different but not quite knowing what different meant. The day of the chapel trip to the seaside dawned and now that he was a bit older, his parents didn't care to go and that was fine with Jimmy and his buddies as they were into all sorts of things that parents knew about but were quite content to look the other way and let somebody else take care of. Jimmy was smoking now because he thought it looked cool and mature but if only he could see himself through other eyes he would have realized he just looked like a lost teenager trying to be a man, but that's part of growing up isn't it? There was singing on the bus, the sun was shining, the elders were explaining what the timetable of events was and none of Jimmy's crowd were taking a blind bit of notice and all Jimmy wanted to know was where Iris was and where she was going to be and who she was going to be with and he intended to be right there with her. There was always a group of them but he managed to stay close to Iris for almost the whole day and the best part of the day was after they had come back from swimming and they just lay about in the sun and he rested his head on her lap and she was okay with that and he wanted time to stand still. He had got over his stumbling and bumbling in her presence but the crush was still right there and he knew how it must look but nothing mattered even when his pals suggested they go to the arcade and play the slot machines, he said no, he just as wanted to be close to her and then he found out that Iris was already going to the same college that he would be going to in September.

September came all too quickly and off he went to college. Jimmy always was one for trying to be prepared for eventualities and possibilities so he had previously taken the bus to Sunderland and timed the walk from the bus station to the college and had looked at the bus schedule for his best choices and he was ever so glad he had taken the time to do this as that first morning, even though he had checked and re-checked his stuff the night before, was nearly a disaster. There was a Sunderland bus which stopped at the top of his road but he figured it most likely would be full and that the majority of the passengers would only be going as far as Chester for their work destinations so he decided he would walk to Chester and get the bus there. Nothing wrong with the idea but it took him longer than he thought to walk down Pelaw Bank and when he got to the bottom he could not believe the line up on the bus stand and not only that, very few passengers got off the bus. There were a couple of routes that the Sunderland buses took and fortunately some people elected to take the other route to him but even so he just made it onto his bus but had to stand for the full nine miles it took to get to Sunderland and it seemed to pick up and drop off people at every stop along the way. College was a real eye opener and no matter how he tried to look or act, he looked like a lost newcomer but at least he was not on his own and after a few weeks he was one of 'them'. This was a time of 'mods' and 'rockers', 'teddy boys' and 'beatniks', drugs and alcohol and sure there were distractions but his upbringing came through and he knew right from wrong although he didn't always exercise the right thing, probably the one thing that kept him on the right path was the dozen or so classmates he had for this new drawing course were all from similar backgrounds and were all new to college and college ways but he was shocked to see Andrew Mackay in the class. This unsettled him a little because he understood that because there were a limited number of places available then there would be no two boys allowed from the same school, let alone the same class. He smelled a rat, certainly the headmaster had not mentioned the possibility of a second student being given the opportunity, in fact, everything had been moved along rather quickly at the time so he suspected that Andrew's father had somehow become acquainted with the college deal and had approached Mr. Anderton and pressured or persuaded the headmaster to see if Andrew could be included, maybe even at the expense of Jimmy being discarded, who knows? and all this must have taken place after the school had closed for the summer holidays. In any event Andrew was in the class, he never ever discussed how he came to be there and as far as Jimmy was concerned, Andrew's father must have some compromising photographs in his possession. You just never know with people do you?

Iris must have had a different schedule or time-table than his because he rarely saw her on the bus but did see her in the cafeteria some days and it became quite obvious she had a boyfriend and never in his life would Jimmy have imagined that Iris, the Iris that he knew, or the Iris that he thought he knew, would have a boyfriend like this jerk. Was he a jerk or was Jimmy just jealous? This smoothy was the best dancer, the coolest looking dude in the college, he obviously could have picked any girl as a partner for his lunchtime jiving sessions but time and again he was to be seen dancing with a beautiful, dusky, hour glass figured girl and what a pair they made, putting on a dancing display for the rabble. How did Iris feel about all of this? Jimmy wanted to go out there in the middle of the floor and demand that he cease and desist or he would get punched on the nose because Iris didn't deserve to be treated like this, but then he realized that it was all just good fun, this was college and he was the one being a jerk and really the whole thing had nothing to do with him but he stopped using the cafeteria for a while until he managed to get his emotions under control. A week or two went by and the regular chapel group were walking home after the Sunday evening service, Iris usually was one of the first to leave the group as her house was closer than the others when Jimmy asked her if he could walk with her, see her home. She said yes, that would be nice and he felt great just being in her company, just like it had been at the seaside trip. He had not actually planned to do this, (or had he?), he was beginning to wonder about himself and thought if he met himself in the Street, would he recognize himself? He heard himself say to Iris, "will you go out with me?" There was like a five-minute silence when nothing happened in the world and they had both stopped walking, she was looking at his flushed face and he knew there was only going to be one answer and Iris said, "I would really, if I was not going out with Joe." Jimmy immediately thought to himself, "bugger Joe," but his face showed absolutely no change of emotion and he even managed to continue the conversation, asking how long they had been going out together and what did she think the future held for her and Joe. They chatted for a long time, even after reaching Iris's house and Jimmy felt better for it. He knew a fair bit about her, that her dad had passed some years previously and that she had two older brothers who were protective of their little sister as only brothers can be. He knew she was a year older than him but found out that she was already into the second year of a four year course at college and then afterwards, who knew where that would take her? A far as Jimmy was concerned, even though the answer had been no, the friendly chat had only served to increase his feelings towards her and although he was able to deal with those feelings, because he had to, they never changed and as the years passed and they went their different ways he often thought about her and was able to make enquiries every so often as to her well-being and he wondered, what if?

Linda remained ever present in his life but he had more or less put her to the back of his mind primarily because she seemed stuck on that boyfriend of hers and although they bicycled together, her boyfriend was now leaning towards motorbikes and Jimmy felt like that he was being left farther and farther behind because he had no interest in motorbikes or any of the things that he thought attracted girls but there were to be a series of circumstances which would result in his and Linda's lives being forever entwined.

Meanwhile at college, he liked being part of the new drawing programme and as the rest of the class were scratching their heads at times, he did not feel out of place when he struggled with some aspect. There was one lad in the class who just seemed a natural, he was a year older than the rest of them but that was not the difference, Dave just seemed to grasp everything so easily. As far as the course agenda requirements were concerned it appears there had been a demand from industry for some time for properly trained engineering or technical illustrators to either work on their own or possibly team up with a technical writer with the task of producing machine spare parts and instruction manuals and this course was the initial attempt to begin to satisfy that demand. Their class instructor had been a draughtsman with years of experience in a large engineering company but had only recently completed his own illustration instruction as far as they knew but what the class liked about the whole set up was everybody was on a first name basis, including the instructor. That was to change soon as the college egg-heads deemed it inappropriate and bordering on familiarity for lecturers and students to be on such an intimate relationship. Jimmy found himself getting involved with students enrolled in other courses in the college, mainly through chatting with them on the bus because there were quite a few who made the daily journey from beyond his hometown and then there were a few who had digs in Sunderland, but as students in general did not have any money these were shared digs and extremely cramped. Nonetheless he found they frequented one pub more than others and as it was obvious he was under age they still found ways to get him a pint or two especially when he expressed interest in going to the college dances with them. He didn't dance much, not that he did not know how to dance, after all, he had learned some dancing at school, his mam and dad went regularly to Old time dances and sister Joan had tried to teach him some Modern Dance steps. Even at chapel, at youth club nights and Christmas parties he had ventured into the new realm of 'bopping' or 'jiving' to the latest rock and roll music, but he enjoyed going to the college dances and persuaded himself that he liked to watch the performers on the floor rather than be a performer himself, although he knew the real reason was that he just did not have the nerve to ask a girl to dance, until one night a girl asked him up to dance, more like she almost dragged him onto the dance floor. This incident changed his outlook and confidence a little but he still wanted to be in the middle of the dance crowd and not around the edge of the floor where people could see him when he was dancing. At those college dances he was introduced to Traditional or Dixieland Jazz type music and he absolutely loved it as all he was into at that time was a bit of Skiffle which his band played and the early rock and roll of Buddy Holly and the Everly Brothers. He loved Buddy Holly and the Crickets and searched out information for all the band members plus in bookstore wanderings he would look for old recordings which there were not too many as Buddy Holly was still a young rising star, but after learning about Traditional Jazz he was hooked and found that not only was it good for listening music but it was excellent for 'jiving' to. The only thing he shied away from, was after the dances finished for the night, groups of students would congregate at some apartment or other and drugs would appear, Jimmy did not know what the drugs were but he saw some of the effects of them. One night when he decided to go to one these after dance parties with a girl he had been dancing with, the party was already in full swing by the time they got there and it didn't take him long to figure that there were one or two shady characters hanging around who just did not appear to be students but the girl he was with wasted no time in contacting one of the undesirables and there was a swift exchange of some sort. She disappeared for a while and when next he saw her she was gyrating madly in the middle of the room and seemed to be giving every guy the 'come-on'. She never even noticed Jimmy again but he had already made up his mind to leave and was making for the door when one of the non-students stopped him and asked where he was going. "Just heading out for some air," said Jimmy and the door stopper said, "Make sure you come back 'cos I've got something for you." Jimmy may have been young in years and younger than most at the party that night but he was no fool and decided then and there that drugs would never be a part of his life even if he had to forego the dances for a while.

He became acquainted with one of the models who posed nude for the 'Life Art' classes in the college as she travelled on the same bus occasionally, this knowledge unsettled him at first when he sat beside her on the bus, his brain would continually try to project images of her without clothes especially when she looked at him and smiled. He wondered if she would still be smiling if she knew what he was thinking, but eventually he never gave it a second thought as it was all just part of normal college life which he was adapting to very fast and liking it. The college Christmas break came and there were no exams to speak of for his class, just some questions and answers to see if everybody had got the hang of the course up to that point but it was obvious that much more was going to be thrown at them in the coming weeks and months. The problem was, and it was an ongoing concern for Jimmy, that it took him far too long to complete anything and some of the things they were being taught, for example, learning how to correctly draw in perspective with calculated vanishing points took time regardless of how fast an individual happened to be, but this was a key element to the course and in time they would no doubt be quite good at it because as they were repeatedly reminded that their potential employer would want to see results on paper and not be in the least interested as to how long it had taken to set up vanishing points.

Rehearsals had been going on for some time for the latest chapel Christmas pantomime offering and Mr. Bellson had excelled himself as usual, he had tremendous imagination and had taken a well-worn story and by weaving his magic, overcoming obvious limitations, he had come up with what promised to be a fun filled 'Aladdin.' He had noticed Jimmy's preference for wearing 'teddy-boy' type clothes and with some sort of idea in mind had cast him in the role of the 'genie'. They had some great times at rehearsal and so much laughter that Mr. Bellson was getting concerned that his players were not going to be ready for the one, and only one, opening night. That night came and the hall was packed and there were the usual panic attacks in the wings and behind the curtain as some of the scenery props were missing and were critical for the show. The 'genie' had a prominent, if at times, lonely part throughout the show but Mr. Bellson had thought it out well and the first appearance of the 'genie', after the lamp had been rubbed as the story goes, caught a few of the audience by surprise. The previous scene ended with the lamp being rubbed, the curtains closed quickly and the lights went out, there was a flash of light and a puff of smoke and suddenly the 'genie' appeared at the front of the stage dressed in a finger-tip long red jacket, purple shirt, bootlace tie, black drainpipe trousers and on his feet were his 'brothel creepers'. His long hair was combed slickly back and his sideburns, which did not match the colour of his hair, were obviously painted on. There had been some debate over the last few weeks about those sideburns because it seemed that 'teddy-boys' sported them but Jimmy could let his beard grow for a month and all he got was a face full of 'bum fluff'. One other reason Mr. Bellson had thought Jimmy was ideal for the part was that his voice did not carry and by standing at the front of the stage and pronouncing, "I am the genie of the lamp and your wish is my command," even those at the rear of the hall would hear him. That was pretty much all he had to say throughout the night, albeit twenty times, but Mr. Bellson had stressed that he take his time in saying his little speech because they needed time back stage to change sets and props. The pantomime was a huge success and much was made at the end of the show in making sure Mr. Bellson was brought on stage and given the ovation he deserved as well as being presented with flowers by one of the girls.

During the previous few weeks he had been having a little trouble with his teeth especially the gap or 'goal posts' in the two front ones as he jokingly referred to them. They would sometimes ache in the cold weather and small pieces would occasionally flake off from trivial exercises like cleaning them and he knew it was only a matter of time before they would come out so he made an appointment to see the dentist to see what could be done. It was still the Christmas holidays and he had a little time before returning to college so he thought that maybe he could have those two front teeth taken out and be fitted with a partial denture and nobody would be any the wiser. Alas, the best laid plans of mice and men....... The dentist was not really a family dentist but the Bland family had all seen him at some time or other and he was okay and an older man so he listened to what Jimmy had in mind then performed his inspection, Yes, he said he could do something along the lines of what Jimmy wanted but his recommendation was that all the teeth be removed because the lack of calcium had weakened them so much that within a year he would begin to lose them at an alarming rate. Jimmy was devastated even when the dentist told him he probably had six good ones at the front, on the bottom, that could be saved and he immediately blurted out, "no way, six months without teeth, I'll not dare go out of the house." Then he added, "what about putting new ones back in the holes," because he had heard of that procedure, even though the very thought of it sent shivers through him but before he said anymore the dentist told him his gums were so small there was absolutely no chance of that working. The dentist said as understandingly as he could, "go home and think about it but I can do the operation two days from now if you want, after that, I am not sure when I can fit you in." Jimmy's mind was made up before he got home, the teeth were out before the end of the week and he was as sick as a dog for three days.

After the winter break, college resumed and the class soon adjusted to seeing Jimmy without his teeth although he did cover his mouth with a scarf most of the time at least for the first few days but he had been correct about the amount of learning to be done in what amounted to not enough time to do it. It is possible, that with the course being new, the powers that be had to exercise some guesswork as to the time required to complete the programme and maybe that would change for future classes but it was hard going for most of the class. Mind you there were one or two that didn't take the instruction seriously enough, not that they didn't have the talent but college in general for them was just an excuse to have a good time. Pretty childish and selfish Jimmy thought as they were denying places to others who would more than welcome the opportunity to learn something new. Ken, the teacher, was always trying to make the subject interesting, draughting and drawing and any sort of art is interesting enough but it is the application that requires some thought and he had been successful in obtaining an old car and a place to keep it. He had arranged for the car to be stripped down as all he and his class were interested in at that point were the mechanical parts, the gearbox, the rear axle and differential mainly, so over the next weeks and months the class would dismantle and label the various parts right down to the nuts and bolts and draw them in an exploded type view as it would be expected to be shown in an auto parts instruction manual. This exercise perked up their attention but couldn't last forever and the results made it clear what was to be expected of them on completion of the course and of course Dave's finished article was just a work of art, even done in pen and ink it showed what could be accomplished. Dave's work and his expertise became the yardstick for the rest of the class and none were ever to match his skill but it was good for the course in general to have that accomplishment which would no doubt be used in the promotion of future classes. February again was marked by another plane crash and this was 'The Day the Music Died' as it became known with deaths of Buddy Holly, Richie Valens and the J. P. Richardson aka 'The Big Bopper'. This too, affected Jimmy as he had followed Buddy Holly's progress and learned a lot of his songs but, as happens a lot of the time, all kinds of new unpublished material suddenly came out and not all of it particularly good music but it sold and the likes of Jimmy bought it. There was one incident in the class that at least brought a couple of laughs and it emphasized the good relationship the class had with Ken. A good many of the lads in the class smoked and it helped that Ken smoked too as he was always up for a smoke break, in fact it was this type of familiarity between students and teachers that had become a bit of a concern to the college authorities who didn't seem to understand that the age gap between college students and college teachers was very small in a lot of cases and this 'familiarity' in no way lessened the importance of the lessons being taught but they did issue a rule that first names were not to be used by students addressing the teacher. The incident was not actually a smoke break, it was early morning before the first lessons and students were either outside or catching up on the latest gossip in the cafeteria but there was always one or two who just had to have a last drag on a cigarette and would take a chance just nipping the end as they were entering the classroom. Fred was one of Jimmy's classmates and a close friend who was always up to tricks and pranks but he had such an innocent cherubic face that usually had people saying, "No, not Fred." Ken was also known for wanting a last smoke before class started so the class was usually assembled and at their drawing boards long before he galloped in, except this memorable morning he was just about on time and got the morning's tasks going immediately. It wasn't too long before he stood up and said, "What's that smell, is somebody smoking?" Nobody said anything but it was obvious that something was burning.

"Fred, are you smoking," Ken continued.

"No sir," said Fred.

"Then what is that smoke haze around your head?' asked Ken.

"Shit, I'm on fire.", shouted Fred

He jumped off his stool desperately patting the hair above his ear while the whole class just erupted with laughter and Fred's face was even more red than usual. Thinking the cigarette was out he had stuck the butt end it behind his ear to be finished later but all he got was singed hair. Fred and Jimmy had a few good times together, they worked at the Post Office as telegram boys during holidays and Fred's house was the scene of some all-night card games, with the approval of his dad of course, and one year they even went on holiday together to a Butlin's Holiday Camp. They were both just turned eighteen at the time, Fred was single, Jimmy was going strong with Hazel but was thinking maybe he should get away on his own while he still could. The first couple of days at the camp were spent at the swimming pool where Fred demonstrated his exceptional skills at swimming and diving. Small wonder Fred's school won most of the annual gala events but he was a bit of a show off and not afraid to advertise his six foot frame and black curly hair. They changed into casual evening clothes, went for supper and that was the last Jimmy saw of him until the evening prior to their departure. Turns out he got shacked up with one of the camp working girls and his remark, "We sat and watched the sun come up every morning", kind of summed up Fred's week, whereas Jimmy spent most of his evenings either in the bar, in the dance hall watching other people dance or playing cards with a bunch who never did anything else but play cards. Not really a holiday for the record books or photograph album and when he bumped into Clive, a younger kid who lived around the corner, Clive wanted to know all the sordid details because in his mind, every boy who went to Butlin's had to have sex as the girls were falling over backwards wanting it and if you didn't get it, then there was obviously something wrong with you. What tourist brochure had he been reading? He pestered Jimmy again and again.

"Did you get anything, did you, did you"?
"No"
"Yes you did, didn't you"?
"No, I didn't".
"But you must have".
"No I didn't".
"I don't believe you".
"Oh fuck off, okay I did".
"I knew it, I knew it".

Jimmy walked away just shaking his head and never thought any more about the incident until a couple of nights later he met Hazel and without so much as a hello it was:

"I hear you were with another girl on your holidays".

"No, not really" replied Jimmy wondering where this was coming from and more importantly where was it going. Then the whole thing came out, Clive had immediately blabbed to his sister, who worked with a friend of Hazel's, who told Hazel. Now he had to back track and plead his innocence, which he did and he was so concerned that he might lose Hazel through this stupid false admission that his genuine honesty came out with his explanation. "Bit sticky for a while there", he thought. It wasn't as if Jimmy didn't have eyes for other girls, he was only human and he knew Hazel had an old flame originating from her schooldays but mostly he kept himself in check even with Fred's sister who he had the 'hots for especially when Fred had set up a tent in the back garden and for a while the two of them were left alone. She was a long-legged beauty and it took all of his attention to keep his hands off her, but he did.

It was while Jimmy and Fred were working at Chester Post Office as telegram boys that an episode occurred which became one of their favourite talking points when reminiscing over a couple of beers. They were always competing with one another, racing to deliver telegrams, running to the bikes in the yard because for the most part the bikes were real bone-shakers and it was difficult to get a good one. Well, this one day Fred was in the lead as they shot out of the yard and into the high street and with both destinations down at the bottom of the street before they parted company it was all systems go. Fred was literally picking up speed because Chester Front Street sloped and as if in slow-motion Jimmy could see ahead that a woman was about to step off the curb in front of Fred. "Don't you fucking dare," he yelled at the top of his voice and it seemed as if the whole street froze in time. As Fred hurtled down the street, Jimmy stopped his bike and just roared with laughter at the look on the woman's face and it was obvious she was not too pleased. They were both fired.

June came and college holidays seemed to differ from the school holidays he remembered, college holidays were longer he was glad to find out and again for Jimmy's class there were no major examinations, they would come next year, but there were the usual basic 'what have you learned' tests and he took the opportunity of taking an English

General Certificate of Education (GCE) examination which was offered for those interested and which he passed before leaving for the summer vacation. The only item on his calendar for that summer was another piano examination which would be his third year of the Royal Conservatory of Music programme under the tutelage of Mr. Armitage. Jimmy had been with Mr.Armitage for a number of years now and the piano teacher's popularity and reputation as a music teacher had not diminished in that time nor had his particularly annoying habit of booking far too many students for what seemed to be the same period for piano lessons especially on Saturday afternoons which had always been Jimmy's lesson time. He already had the date and time for his examination, which was always held in Newcastle and he proceeded to the place with a little anxiety because now as part of the examination he would be asked to identify notes as played on the piano and in addition he would be asked to sing particular notes, all in addition to playing the required pieces with some degree of accuracy and demonstrating his ability to perform scales with either hand and then with both hands together in an acceptable fashion. His voice had broken some time previously but that was not the problem, Jimmy just could not sing. He wasn't bad at recognizing notes and keys and timing but just did not have the confidence to stand up and let fly, as the saying goes. He underestimated his abilities as usual and passed the examination, no small feather in his cap and so later that summer he went for his piano lesson on a particularly lovely Saturday afternoon. Did Jimmy think he deserved better after his success in the examination? Actually, the thought never entered his head but what did bother him as he entered the waiting room reserved for students waiting their turn was the number of students already there. He had gone early expecting a bit of a wait but there had to be four or five ahead of him. One or two he knew from his school days but a quick calculation told him he was not going to get out of there in time to go home, get changed and be back down to Chester in time to meet his date. Maybe some of them in the room were not there for a full lesson, and he asked the question but no, they were all there for a full lesson and to add insult to injury somebody else came in. He sat there and stewed and time dragged on and nothing was happening and you could swear there was steam starting to blow out of his ears. He asked Judith and Dave again if they had their lesson time right and of course they said yes, they had and that Jimmy should know better after all this time than to make arrangements for a Saturday night. Well, that comment didn't go down well at all but he let it go and decided that for now he was okay for time, so he would just wait and see how things panned out. Half an hour passed and then another half hour and only one person had gone in and in that same time two newcomers had arrived. Another half hour passed and Jimmy figured if he waited any longer there was no chance of his meeting his date and he also realized that in his present state of agitation he was not really up for a piano lesson. "Jesus Christ," he thought, "why does he do this?" He thought he heard Mr. Armitage's study door open so he jumped up and charged out of the waiting room into the large hall but the study door was closed so he knocked once on the study door and barged in. The look on Mr. Armitage's face was priceless, but only for a moment, he did have a student with him but Jimmy was oblivious to this, he only had eyes for the teacher and he demanded to know why Mr. Armitage took on so many students for the same time period and did he know that it was Saturday afternoon and Jimmy wasn't the only one to be kept waiting for hours and it was time somebody told Mr. Armitage a few home truths. It was a large study with a beautiful grand piano in the center of the room of what was a well maintained, large, nice but old house on a huge corner lot. Must cost a fortune to keep, Jimmy had thought during one of his previous visits. "Get out," screamed Mr. Armitage," and do not ever come back, you are finished, absolutely finished here and everywhere else, I'll make sure you will never get another lesson in this town, do you understand, you ungrateful imbecile," Jimmy just took one last look at him, gave him the finger and said, "up yours, pal".

He had figured his mam would be really in a snit with him over the piano thing, especially when he told her that he was finished with the piano lessons but to his amazement she just said she had seen it coming for some time. Aren't mams just unbelievable? But he did sense some disappointment in her remarks and looks and Lizzie just hoped that her son had not been too outspoken with Mr. Armitage because word would soon come back to her. His band was still getting the occasional gig and they were still practicing mostly in their own homes but they were getting better and later that year, during the winter they got a gig at a youth club in Fatfield. So they loaded their stuff on to the bus and off they went. It was a bone chilling, freezing cold night and Jimmy could not seem to get his fingers warm but they set up on the stage, rehearsed a couple of numbers and then waited for their call to go on. They all decided they needed a pee before they started, no problem, there was a small bathroom just down the corridor, just a toilet and a sink, that was okay except there was no light bulb in the light fixture. But that was okay too, the four of them took their places around the toilet bowl while the door was open just enough for some light to show, then they memorized their positions and where they were supposed to aim and the door was closed to prevent prying eyes. Good plan, in theory, but as Jimmy realized from the get go somebody wasn't peeing according to script. The door was opened and the front of Jimmy's trousers were soaked and it was Colin who had been opposite him and Jimmy was furious while the others just howled with laughter at his appearance. He was beside himself and he turned to Colin and shouted, "fuckin' hell Colin, couldn't you point you dick downwards like everybody else? Think it's a big fuckin' joke or what?" Then they were called to go on stage where Jimmy had to hold his guitar lower down to try and cover the front of his pants which were literally starting to steam. Anybody asking him afterwards about songs they sang that night would just get a dumb stare as the rest of the night for Jimmy was just a nightmare. Coming home on the bus his pants were starting to stiffen, it was so cold and as he got off the bus he said to the rest of the band, "I'm finished, that's the last time I will ever play with you guys," and he knew at the same time he was saying the words that was not what he wanted. But it <u>was</u> the last time he played with them and shortly afterward he swapped his guitar for a tennis racquet and gave his splendid one thousand plus stamp collection away and those two decisions he regretted for the rest of his life.

The next few months at college were a real test for Jimmy, he knew some of his classmates were also having a difficult time but he imagined that no one was struggling as much as him. It was not just the stuff to be learned but the time they were given to accomplish drawing tasks, there were pencil drawings and sketches, ink work on a special type of board and air brush work which he had a particularly hard time mastering and then there was the preparation for the big examination coming up. The examination, the class had been informed, would be spread over three days and would comprise of a Friday test lasting four hours, and on the following day, a test lasting six hours and the following Saturday another six hours. These times may seem long but Jimmy knew he would need all the time available for him to complete the work and of course they did not know exactly what was going to be on the examination papers. Ken realized the class needed a break and he had authorized a half day holiday for them so some of the class, along with some other classmates had arranged to go to Roker beach or if they had time up to Seaburn which was nicer. On the day they all brought their swimming gear except Jimmy who had forgotten all about it. "Not to worry," said Dave, "I live just up the road, I'll get you a spare pair." So that was how Jimmy came to be wearing Dave's swimming trunks but not before some bright spark stole Jimmy's trousers from under the bathroom door as he was changing and he had to make his way into the main hall to retrieve them. The bright spark, he suspected was Matty who was always into some kind of mischief, like the time he and Jimmy decided to go to a Wednesday night Sunderland football game at Roker Park. Because there was time to kill after college closed and before the game started, Matty decided they should get onto Roker pier despite Jimmy's objections that the pier was closed and fenced off with barbed wire. The tide was in and waves were pounding the walls of the pier and to physically get onto the pier they had to climb upwards and out over water and then get over the barbed wire without castrating themselves. Matty didn't have a problem but Jimmy did, though he would not let Matty see his desperation and absolutely refused to let Matty get the better of him. Anyway, off they went to the beach, a mixed bunch if ever there was one, and it was not a particularly warm day, even with the sun out, the wind coming off the North Sea cooled everything down. That didn't deter some of the more hardy souls who quickly shed their clothes and ran into the waves. Not Jimmy though, he was absolutely frozen and was as slow as he could be in getting his togs off, but he didn't want to look too bad in front of the women so eventually he was ready and decided to just stand for a moment to collect his thoughts. The voice came from Maureen who was sitting beside him and she said, "it's a good job I'm broad minded," Jimmy looked down at his swimming trunks which were wide open at the sides instead of the snug fit that was supposed to be. He should have known and checked, especially with Dave being six foot two and one hundred eighty pounds but the theft of his trousers had put his mind in chaos. Despite the cold he went as red as beetroot and charged into the sea but was out seconds later shivering so much his knees knocked together but he didn't care what he looked like by that time.

The June examination date approached and he thought the best thing he could do was try and prepare a portfolio of presentation drawings which he would be able to show prospective employees, as it became obvious, and it had never been a stipulation of the college, that there would be no assistance in gaining employment, with or without the examination success. Jimmy should have had more confidence in his ability because he did have that ability but he almost always convinced himself that he was just not up to the task and this would be an ongoing trait and up to that point in his life his mam had quietly pushed and guided him and mostly she had been able to get him to hold his head up and get him to believe he was equal to any task. Maybe the fact that situations bothered him to such an extent was a good thing because it showed he cared about the direction his life was taking him and in which direction he was determined to go but when things got the better of him he would retreat into his own world of books, music and games in the confines of his home or even his own bedroom, he may have not realized but this did not go unnoticed by his family or friends.

The examination results came out, only Dave passed and that was no real surprise but there was genuine concern from some and the parents of one student came to the college and demanded that their son be found a job and that surely a mistake had been made in the examination assessment, quite a scene actually. "Welcome to the real world", thought Jimmy. College had certainly been an experience but could that time have been spent more wisely, maybe good job opportunities had been missed while at college or would the technical illustration course, albeit without the examination success, be a factor in gaining employment that would not have been open without it? All Jimmy knew was that he was sixteen years old, almost seventeen and he did not have a job and he may have blown his chances of getting any kind of apprenticeship. These disappointments did not stop him from going to the end of term college dance where he renewed some acquaintances beforehand who were hanging out in the usual pub and didn't seem to mind getting him a couple of pints before the dance. One special girl acquaintance made him forget all about his disappointments when she invited him round to her flat long before the dance finished, so he had time to get the last bus home. "Ain't college great", he thought, "some people have no inhibitions".

He knew his mam and dad would be supportive as best they could but he felt bad at the thought he had let them down after all the sacrifices they had made for him and he had failed. Well, he thought, later on after the disappointment of the examination results had stopped bothering him, I will not let them down, so he made a hardboard carrying case for his portfolio of drawings, some of which were quite large which made the carrying case quite heavy, then he planned out his route for every day of the week to go in person to every establishment in the district as well as mailing off letters requesting an interview to prospective employers, and on the first Monday after finishing college he set off, using public transport and shanks' pony as his mode of travel but he was used to that.

Like everything else that is new and different, the initial excitement and energy available for a new venture is boundless but this endeavor of his was a hard slog even for a young person and the responses he received were not encouraging. For starters, there were not many establishments too keen to put out the welcoming mat for some kid knocking on their door unannounced asking for a job or at least asking for an interview with the possibility of obtaining employment. A lot of the responses were, "we are not hiring at this time,", or, "mail in a request for an application form," or "here is an application form for you to complete and submit," or, "get lost." No, that last one was not an actual response but it certainly had the same meaning a lot of the time. And so it went on week after week, Monday through Friday with his weekends spent filling out application forms or writing interview requests and suddenly it was already into August. A few miles north of Chester, just before reaching Newcastle and just off the A1 road was the Team Valley Trading Estate which came under the jurisdiction of Gateshead, an industrial town on the south side of the River Tyne, this trading estate consisted of a large diverse complex of factories and offices and had been the main focus of Jimmy's enquiries. The bus would take him to the southern end of the estate and then he would walk, with his portfolio of drawings, which he swore got heavier every day, the full length of the complex, venturing off in other directions if he saw a possible opportunity. By August, not only was he dispirited but he was absolutely, physically knackered and was seriously thinking about throwing in the towel as he knew that September was the time when new college terms began and new hires were more likely to be well established prior to new terms beginning. There it was again, the time factor which seemed to have a recurring theme in Jimmy Bland's life. School wasn't too bad compared to this he was thinking. Not one for giving up easy and after a weekend's rest, if it could even remotely be called rest, he set off again on the Monday morning with his carrying case of drawings, at least the weather was good and had been kind to him over the last few weeks., but boy was he tired. Tuesday came and went and on the Wednesday he decided to backtrack on some places where he thought he had had a positive feeling, you know, sometimes you get an instinct or maybe he was just getting desperate but he remembered passing a particular place, not even knocking on the door of this place because there didn't appear to be an obvious front door but on closer inspection he figured where it must be. Kind of a nondescript place, with what looked like two story offices at the front with a factory type building to the side and rear. The building was actually at the south end of the trading estate, almost opposite where the bus dropped him off every morning and he thought, "bugger it, if this comes to nowt, I'm off home on the next bus," and so he went inside. There was a small reception area with a receptionist on duty and although it was getting late in the afternoon it was nowhere near quitting time he figured, so there was no reason for her to be looking at her watch. He explained the reason for his visit and she made a phone call, "that's a good start," Jimmy thought but he knew better than to let his hopes build up, after all he was a seasoned campaigner now. "Mr. Dryden, the Drawing Office Manager will see you now," the receptionist said. Jimmy must have looked like a dork standing there with his mouth open, trying to grasp what the young lady had just said, when she spoke again, "he's not got all day you know, up those stairs, his office is the first door on the left." He collected his wits as well as his portfolio, stammered a thank you and negotiated the stairs, just hesitating for a moment outside Mr. Dryden's office, then knocking on the door. "Come in," he heard and his immediate reaction on entering was, "this place stinks," but it was only a fleeting thought, it was the smell of roll-your-own cigarettes he remembered later and the little blighter was almost a chain smoker. There were the usual pleasantries as they introduced themselves and fortunately for Jimmy he was beginning to settle down as he realized that this may be his big chance, maybe his only chance, so he described his schooling and education experience, mentioning his recent drawing course at the college which Mr. Dryden expressed some interest in and he asked to see some of his work. There was not much room in the office and the desk was cluttered with all kinds of stuff, papers, notes and drawings but there was small side table on which Jimmy started placing his best work, giving a brief description of each. He was careful not to go overboard and risk boring Mr. Dryden with useless details as he was prone to do on occasion and then it was obvious Mr. Dryden had seen enough as he asked Jimmy to sit down and proceeded to explain what life was like in the real world. At first Jimmy thought it was a dismissal lecture but the Drawing Office Manager was attempting to educate Jimmy about life in industry and the requirements and obligations of employees and did Jimmy think he was up to the task of committing the next few years of his life to achieving some engineering experience. Jimmy's head was in a whirl by this time and just hoping that his answers were the right ones because this whole meeting had taken on a different aspect, a different direction, than he had anticipated. Then he heard Mr. Dryden say, "thank you Mr. Bland, it was a pleasure meeting with you, we'll be in touch." He wandered out of the office and down the stairs in a complete daze, the receptionist said, "bye", Jimmy heard nothing. There was a bus stop just along a bit and he waited and waited and eventually a bus came but he realized afterwards that buses were scheduled to run at factory closing times. So much to learn! But at least this was promising, as he had not even had a glimmer of hope up to this point and so he, just a little bit, mentioned it to his mam and dad when he got home and of course they were over the moon and Jimmy found himself having to deflate their enthusiasm and optimism as much as he wanted to be part of the celebration. He had only been in an interview, for goodness sake, come on down to earth, he told himself, it'll turn out to be nothing, but secretly he had never been so excited and the very next day he was at the mailbox. "What are you doing"? He told himself, "get a grip and get on with your life, you still have things to do". But it was no good, he went over and over again every word that had been spoken during the interview, trying to identify words that could be interpreted as being positive indications of a job offer and really ignoring all the other negative indications. He was worrying himself sick he realized. The days rolled by and Jimmy managed to make himself useful, helping around the house and performing a couple of gardening tasks for his mam's friends, he even managed to sit at the piano for thirty minutes and run through a couple of pieces, much to the delight of his mam. About a week went by after the interview and there was a letter for him, he had been out most of the afternoon on his bike and there was only his mam in the house when he returned and she had left the letter on the table where he could not possibly miss it, and he saw it immediately. He casually took off his cycling gear and proceeded to store his bike in the hall, wiping it down a little, Lizzie had stopped whatever she had been doing and waited patiently and waited and waited and eventually Jimmy could not dither any longer so he pounced on the letter and ripped it open.

> "Dear Mr. Bland,
> Thank you for your interest in employment with our company. We are pleased to offer you the position of Apprentice Junior Mechanical Draughtsman. As part of your duties you will be required to go school one day per week to study for your Mechanical Engineering Certificates along with other duties as per the Apprenticeship Programme. Please report to Mr. Dryden on such and such a date at 9am.........."

Jimmy read and re-read the first two sentences again and again, not even seeing or digesting the last few lines. Lizzie didn't have to ask, she knew by the look on his face where a broad smile was starting to form and she was so happy for him she could have cried, so much work, so much effort and so much heartbreak but she knew it would not be easy for him and neither she nor Eddie would be able to give him much help with his studies. There were some other important details in the letter, he realized later, like how much he would be making, hours of work and the like but he did not care about trivial things just then although he did make a note of the date he was expected to report and it was not too far away.

CHAPTER 7

Joining the Workforce

It was a case of grow up and grow up fast for Jimmy Bland as he reported for work on his first day and the first thing he made sure of was that he was not late. Mr. Dryden's office still stunk of roll-your-own cigarettes Jimmy noticed straight away as he faced him across his untidy desk that bright and sunny morning. The Drawing Office Manager was very pleasant as he welcomed the new hire but Jimmy suspected there was another, not so pleasant side to him which he hoped he would never see so he listened intently to what his boss was telling him. Years before, when welding was in its infancy, one of the many companies involved in the initial design of welding equipment had introduced a successful application and like all initial developments the company needed funds to market the design. Successive take-overs and buy-outs had taken place over the years with the result that the company Jimmy was now employed by became a fabrication arm of a much bigger concern with the head office located elsewhere in the country. This design and fabrication company's main purpose in the industry was to design and build special purpose machines upon which could be mounted appropriate welding equipment, depending on the weld process required, with which to automatically weld structures or pressure vessels for the process equipment industry, the key word being 'automatically'. "So don't be confused or misled by the 'Welding Company' name out front," said Mr. Dryden. He also went on to explain to Jimmy that although he appreciated his talent as a Technical Illustrator the company did not, at that time, have sufficient work of that type to employ him on a full-time basis, hence the Apprentice Junior Mechanical Draughtsman offer with the demands and rewards that that training offered but he would be required to produce illustrations as and when required. "Holy Shit", thought Jimmy, "two for the price of one, this little rascal's no fool is he"? Mr. Dryden went on to say that Jimmy was enrolled at Gateshead Technical College starting September for one day per week and his course would be S1 First Year Ordinary National Certificate in Mechanical Engineering and the lads in the office would advise him what books he would need. "I'll get John to show you where your drawing board and desk are and he will help get you settled in, good luck." John did just that and introduced him to the rest of the drawing office staff which was made up of about a dozen draughtsmen with their drawing boards, situated in two rows with a central aisle, two lady tracers, three of four apprentices and two or three clerical staff at the back. Jimmy was overwhelmed by all that was happening and what he had been told and as quickly as he was introduced to one person he promptly forgot the name, another problem he was constantly aware of. After he dumped his stuff on his desk, he was told to go to the Personnel Office to finalize and sign some papers and he would find it by going through the door next to Mr. Dryden's office, down the corridor, through the typing pool area and the office was on the left. Well, on entering the typing pool area he was greeted with whistles and comments and his face was getting redder and redder, the door at the other end seemed miles away but he somehow made it and he said to himself, "there's no chance I'm coming back this way," but of course there was no other way and being a little more prepared for the return journey he even managed a smile which did not go unnoticed by some. Later in the day he got to tour the rest of the facility including the factory which was a lot bigger than he had imagined from the outside and where, he had been told, he would be spending some time as part of his apprenticeship training.

September was indeed not too far away, Jimmy took his list of required text books and other supplies he had been advised to buy and made a point of getting the bus to Gateshead Tech. as everyone called it and although it was closed for the summer he got a good general idea of the layout of the place and its location relative to where he was working and it proved to be within walking distance, bit of a slog uphill from the Valley but a manageable thirty minutes hike. The Newcastle bus, which Jimmy used quite frequently, went right past the college so that was not going to be a problem. It was only if he ended up taking a night class that he would have to walk to the college from work, as one or two of the other lads were doing. The first week at work flew by and he knew he was being given time to adjust but he also knew that there were tough times ahead and he would have to learn the ropes fast but it seemed like the other lads were eager to help providing he asked for help and not fiddle and fart around as he sometimes did when he was a bit unsure. So this was his introduction to the work force and Jimmy was to look back many times during his life to the nearly six years he spent at the 'Welding Company' and realize just how fortunate he had been, the technical knowhow that had been afforded him, the friends he had made, the education he had received, the social activities he had been involved with, all providing the basis for a well-paid future wherever he chose to go.

  Technical College proved extremely difficult for him, it became clear that most of the class had had that additional year of schooling until they were sixteen and then went straight into apprenticeship programmes, whereas Jimmy left school at fifteen and had spent a year and a half learning the new drawing course. He struggled with even the refresher lessons at the beginning of the course which were designed just as starter materials meant to get the student back into the school environment, and of course there were the dreaded examinations at the end of each year, whose results were sent to the employer for his assessment of progress and it was not unheard of for employees to be fired for poor or failed marks, after all, firms were laying out a fair amount of money for these young men. "Holy shit," Jimmy said to himself early on, "I'm never going to be able to manage this."

A NOT QUITE A GEORDIE STORY

He found relief as usual in his cycling and football but had not been doing much of either as of late and other than a couple of dates with girls that he knew from school he was aware that he needed to get out a bit more. His mates from around where he lived mentioned they had not seen him for a while and was he okay? It is so easy to disappear from view isn't it? When what is really required is the opposite and he remembered that one of the lads had said there was a dance on at Chester ballroom every Monday night and he could go with a bunch of them or they would see him down there so off he went with his suit on and his shoes polished. The place was packed and he could barely move without bumping into someone he knew, there was a disc jockey playing the latest music and the floor was full of dancers doing their thing, mostly girl partnering girl Jimmy noticed but he was content to watch, not being able to dance this new stuff and he suspected that most of the lads couldn't dance either. He met a pal he had not seen for a long time even though they lived on the same street but having gone to different schools they had drifted apart and Bob said why don't you come down to the Welfare Club? He was referring to the Pelaw Colliery Miners' Welfare Club at the bottom of Pelaw Bank which was run by two local Pelaw chaps where there was a snooker table upstairs and a gym downstairs and with a small fee you could become a member. Bob hadn't said what nights he went but that didn't matter, Jimmy just wandered down one night when he wasn't doing anything in particular and ventured into the snooker room. There was one table in a fairly small room especially for snooker purposes with some bench seating around the walls, the place was packed and everyone was smoking, or so it seemed. There was literally a permanent haze over the table and notices everywhere which said 'No Cigarettes on the Table'. Which was kind of awkward because that was about the only place you could put a cigarette, except keep it in your mouth. Jimmy enjoyed a cigarette but that room was no place for him so he went in search of the gym downstairs. It was small but well laid out and equipped with a box and a vaulting horse, mats, some weights and a makeshift boxing ring. There were a few lads about but not much going, looked like a dead night, Jimmy thought when one of the two men who ran the place came over to speak to him. "My name's Joe," he said by way of introduction, "interested in joining the boys' club?" he asked. Jimmy said yes, he was interested but explained that he hadn't done much of anything in a gym before although when he left school he had been quite good on the pommel horse he admitted. Joe gave him some membership details and the nights for various activities although he could come down any night if he wanted to. Then Joe said, "you Eddie Bland's lad?" Jimmy nodded, "figured I'd seen you around, your mam and dad are friendly with the Bennets aren't they, I know the Bennets well." Joe had seen Jimmy eying the boxing ring, so he said, "interested in boxing or learning to box?" Jimmy said he might be although the thought had never entered his head and Joe followed up with, "you could do with beefing up a bit, bit of a challenge maybe, but we probably could do something with you." Jimmy thought, "what the heck, it could be beneficial someday". He thanked Joe for the chat and said he would give all that information some thought and he would come down again when he had made his mind up. He had always reckoned he was not a bad little scrapper but his size compared to the other guy's usually made his decision whether to fight or walk away. An interesting thing had happened when he had met Bob at the dance that other night, Bob had introduced him to some of his pals, none of whom Jimmy knew, again, different schools probably being the reason, they were mostly a friendly lot, though there were one or two who seemed to be quite capable of looking after themselves in any kind of situation and he had thought at the time it may not be a bad idea to get in with a good bunch of lads especially if he were to get into the odd spot of trouble when his temper flared, so eventually that's what happened, he became one of the lads. There was Bob, Ray, Dick, Chris, Maverick ('cos he was tall and dark), Flash (so nicknamed "cos he was slow), Nick and Tommy. That was the usual crowd, although there were one or two fringe members as well. Saturday nights became their night at the wrestling in Newcastle, dabbling in under-age drinking, getting tossed out of pubs and getting into the occasional scrap after the dance. But prior to all that he decided to take out membership at the Miners' Welfare and met again with Joe to pay his dues and get some more information. It was while Joe was in the office attending to some paperwork that a lad, whom Jimmy recognized from somewhere, made some comment regarding Jimmy's thin frame and pasty face and kind of jostled him, catching him slightly off balance, much to the amusement of this other lad who remarked, "you'll be no fuckin' good here, we don't play tiddlywinks." Without even realizing, Jimmy swung around, reached out and grabbed the lad by the front of his shirt and his fist ended up one inch away from the lad's nose. Joe rushed out of the office shouting, "let's have none of that here, if you wanna fight, there's the ring, apologize to each other right now and shake hands." Joe took Jimmy into the office and said, "I don't like that kind of stuff but it happens, especially with Sammy, who has his own way of welcoming new members, you'll find he'll be okay with you now." Joe had noticed in Jimmy that aggressiveness which sometimes surfaced and he remarked that maybe if they worked at it and controlled it, along with some exercises he may become a good little boxer. Jimmy said, "it's no good being a good boxer if the other guy is a fighter," to which Joe replied, "everything in good time son."

Jimmy had a few weeks at his new job to try and learn as much as he could about drawing office protocol and procedures before the dreaded September day when he had to go to college. To say that everything was a challenge was an understatement, even the drawing board seemed huge with this horizontal thing which was supposed to be moved up and down and positioned on this horizontal thing were different sized set squares for drawing vertical and angular lines and there was a kind of trough thing attached to the bottom of the board where you could leave your pencils and erasers. Actually it was not all that bad as he had used similar equipment during the drawing course but it just seemed different and it also seemed to him that everybody was watching him and it didn't take long for the comments to start, especially from the younger tracer, Margaret, scoffing about the way he pronounced certain words. He had forgotten about the 'Geordie' issue and how some people didn't care one way or the other and yet for some it seemed to be a big thing, and it was a big thing with Margaret as she would not let one minute pass without making some remark. What made it worse was that everybody in the office was from the Tyneside area and as it was obvious he would not be getting any support there, he just went along with the good natured banter but secretly he was attempting to pronounce those few 'Geordie' words as they did, but it did not come natural and if he got mad, which was more than once, everything just went right out of the window and then he would upset everyone including himself. He contented himself with looking at Margaret's legs as she sat there perched on her stool as her drawing board was three places directly behind his and all he had to do was turn around, so he told her, "every time you make a stupid remark I'm going to turn around." Probably shouldn't have said that he thought later 'cos she did have a nice pair of legs and boobs to go with them. There were similar episodes when he started Gateshead College as his class was full of 'Townies' as his dad called them but once the novelty wore off, then it was okay, except for one lad, Brown was his name and he was the class smart-arse. He was loud and he picked on the quieter lads just for fun but there was never any doubting his ability to learn quickly. He singled out Jimmy and gave him a hard time at the beginning and all the way through the course and made no exception when Jimmy passed and showed up the following year he would yell, "hey Blandy, never thought you would be back." The other lad Brown picked on was Albert, who also worked at Jimmy's place. Albert was smart beyond his years, but quiet and maybe a bit odd, he lived close to the college but was always late. The difference between Albert and Jimmy was, Albert never let anything or anybody bother him, even the time when he forgot his slide rule during an important examination, he calculated everything long-hand or used logarithmic tables and still finished the examination thirty minutes before the closest student and then he asked to leave so he could go back to work.

Jimmy realized he now had some money in his pocket but his mam had already assessed the situation and asked him one day if he would consider paying his board rather than him turning over his pay packet every week and she dishing out his pocket money. Parents are always one step ahead aren't they? Maybe it's because they have been around a bit longer, you think? Jimmy thought it was a great idea until a few weeks went by and he needed some clothes and books and then maybe it was not such a good idea but it was teaching him responsibility and managing his finances and he could always ask his dad for a loan couldn't he? As the weeks at work and college progressed, things did not really get any easier for him, trying to absorb all the new stuff especially the engineering subjects which he was being taught at the college on that one day per week. Some of the lads in the class actually saw that one day at school as being a holiday as they seemed to have no problem at all with the questions and homework but Jimmy was concerned because this was only the first year and no doubt it would get a lot tougher. Just for a little break at work, he longed for the boss to come along and ask him to do some illustrations for an instruction manual or something, anything, just to be able to show everybody what he was capable of, but it was to be a while before that happened.

Jimmy had met a girl at the Chester Ballroom dance, her name was Betty and they were getting along okay, the only downside to the relationship was that Betty was from Stanley, about a half hour's bus ride from Chester. He knew Stanley fairly well having cycled through and around the area many times and he knew where the Stanley Palais dance hall was, only reason he was thinking about that was because Betty and her friends went there when they chose not to go to Chester, Jimmy thought Stanley Palais was a dump but he kept that to himself and he knew the girls preferred Chester Ballroom any day, maybe it was the Chester lads they preferred as well he thought, but he kept that thought to himself also. Betty seemed quite happy to come down to Chester not just for the dances as they occasionally went to the movies or just walked depending on the weather but even so it was no real surprise to Jimmy when she suggested he come up to Stanley for the next Monday night dance at the Palais. He didn't have a problem with that so he said okay and on the night he was up there about seven thirty. Betty was waiting for him outside the dance hall and they went in together, actually not too bad he thought, although he knew it would fill up later on. He was introduced to some of Betty's friends who eyed him up and down, forming girly opinions, no doubt, he thought, well, nothing to stop me eying them up and down either. They had a few dances and it was obvious Betty was well known and well liked and that made Jimmy feel good and he began to slowly relax and enjoy himself but come around nine or nine thirty the place really started to fill up and he thought oh, oh, the lads are coming out of the pubs with their Dutch courage and stinking of beer. Sure enough, suddenly it was not so enjoyable, he obviously couldn't stop Betty from dancing with some other guy, if he asked for a dance but it became more frequent and he overheard a comment or two from one jerk in particular who remarked to his buddies about having a Chester lad in their midst. Jimmy thought," time to call it a night", and asked Betty if he could walk her home, she seemed put out at first and began to argue then said okay let's go, much to Jimmy's relief as he could sense some change in the atmosphere around him. Anyway he walked her home, they did some major snogging around the back of her house and Jimmy told her he had really enjoyed the night but he had been getting one or two looks from some of lads, one in particular, Betty said not to worry about him, he was just a little jealous and would Jimmy come up to Stanley again? He said of course but it would not be a regular weekly thing, 'cos he had an idea where this conversation was going. So for a few weeks they exchanged visits between Chester and Stanley and they were really getting to know one another well and liking their get-togethers until one night they had a bit of a tiff, probably a bit more of a tiff, he thought later, and the mistake he made was letting the night end badly instead of trying to make amends. Betty missed the next Chester dance and Jimmy was disappointed but there she was on the next Monday so he made a point of trying to resolve things, which he did and asked her to come down to watch a midweek movie with him which he really wanted to see and he thought she would enjoy too, so the arrangements were made. She stood him up. No girl had ever stood him up in his life. He was absolutely pissed. Okay he thought, something happened, something came up unexpected, nothing to be alarmed about, what I will do is go up to the Stanley dance at the next opportunity and see if she's there and then we'll have a chat. That's what he did and Betty was there, surrounded by her girlfriends as usual but there were a few lads hanging about who suddenly seemed to have an interest in the proceedings. He caught her eye and motioned for her to move over to the side where they could talk, she moved over but he could sense a coldness that was never there before so he launched into his prepared speech. Finally she agreed to come down to Chester the following Wednesday and they would go to the pictures even though the sense of indifference was still there he thought maybe everything could still be okay. Wednesday night came and whenever he thought about it later on, which he did many times, he could not believe what he did, he stood Betty up. Never in his worst thoughts would he ever believe he would do that to a girl, whatever the circumstances, tit for tat, you got me so I'll get you type of thing, that was strictly for kids, he knew he had done wrong and was so bothered about his actions and what she would think of him that the following Friday night he took the early bus up to Stanley and went to Betty's house. Her mother said she had gone to the dance and if you were Jimmy, she did not want to see you. Doesn't make any difference now Jimmy thought and made for the dance. He paid for his ticket and the place was packed but he had no difficulty in locating Betty, she was surrounded, as usual, by her crowd of friends both male and female but common sense just seemed to fly out the window when Jimmy was like this as he went straight over to her and asked for a quiet word and didn't they owe that much to each other? He actually surprised himself, considering the mood he was in, finding the right words and saying he was sorry and could they not pick up the pieces and get back to where they had been before any of this bad stuff had happened but Betty was not interested and kept glancing over to her friends, none of the glances were lost on Jimmy and he was now thinking of just getting out of there. What a pity, he thought, and no real explanation, and then he thought, "why the fuck do I bother with these girls, they're just a problem as if I didn't have enough on my plate." All the time he was thinking, he was calculating the distance to the exit, because he hadn't come too far into the hall but his path of escape was gradually being cut off by the 'Stanley Wankers' as he was to refer to the Stanley lads forever afterwards. If just that one shit-head who was making all the noise was to come forward I could try out my new found boxing skills but he knew in the real world that did not happen and Jimmy suspected that tonight 'prudence would be the better part of valour'. Betty was also aware of the trouble brewing and she really had no desire to see Jimmy get hurt because of her but she also knew what some of those Stanley boys were capable of so she said to him, "there's another way out of here, I'll tell everybody that you and I need some time to talk, well take a walk and I'll show you where to go." Jimmy never did see Betty again nor did he ever visit Stanley again, either on his bike or by bus, but he often thought, as most kids do, that maybe, just maybe, things could have been much different.

He realized and decided he needed to put things in perspective and found it was okay to discuss certain things with his mam and dad so he knuckled down to the business of learning and keeping fit and healthy as much as time allowed. He had the type of features that reflected any stress he may be feeling, maybe lack of sleep or just sometimes being a bit under the weather and people would remark and show concern for his well-being occasionally, and he did remember one time the headmaster from his senior school years asking his mam, "does Jimmy get enough sleep Mrs. Bland?" No doubt based on the way he looked on a Monday morning after listening to Radio Luxembourg top twenty until midnight the previous night. He figured to give it a good shot until Christmas at least and then he would get a break like everyone else.

Life really does have some strange twists and turns and Jimmy's thoughts of Linda, Iris, Betty and a few others would soon be a thing of the past when he met and was introduced to Linda's cousin, Hazel. This happened at Christmas time, his first Christmas after starting work at the 'Welding Company' and his first holiday break from the technical college. Over the years, Linda's parents and Jimmy's parents had formed a bond of friendship which particularly blossomed at Christmas time. Even though times could be tough and people just as tough in the North East of England especially with the current coal mining disputes pitting friend against friend and neighbour against neighbour, Christmas was special to just about everyone and so a party had been arranged at Linda's parent's house. The gathering was really an adults' get together, with the kids being brought along probably so the parents could keep tabs on them, if the truth was known.

Fortunately the council houses were fairly big with three bedrooms, a good size sitting room and an eat-in kitchen so the younger ones were quick to take over the kitchen and leave the grown-ups the sitting room. When Jimmy got there, Linda's boyfriend was already there, seemed like he had been there for ages, Jimmy could never put his finger on the reason, but as much as they were the same age, had similar interests, there was just something about this lad that bothered him, being a little jealous of his relationship with Linda obviously didn't help matters did it? Anyway there were still people to come and shortly after the Bland family arrived, Linda's cousin Hazel came in with her parents. Linda's mam and Hazel's man were sisters but all the years Jimmy had known Linda he had never met or he could not remember meeting Linda's aunt and certainly he was not aware of Hazel's existence Hazel was a good bit younger than Jimmy but there was an instant spark, for want of a better word, a mutual awareness, a definite 'hello there'. Linda spotted the connection straight off, maybe she had orchestrated the whole thing, women can be so devious, or has nobody noticed? The night had not gone too far on when Hazel said 'yes' to Jimmy's suggestion they go down to his parent's place to watch a Beatles show which was on television, nothing to do with the fact that there was nobody in his parents' house, which would have most certainly derailed those plans had he thought about asking his or her parents for permission. Linda said she would tell anyone who asked, that they had gone for a walk but had better not be too long or they would all be in big trouble. Jimmy had no bad intentions, he did really want to see the Beatles show and in any case Hazel looked a bit young but they found an easiness talking to one another and chatted away constantly and as the show was not all that good they soon decided to head back, just in case they had been missed. Just as well they did because Hazel's mam had been asking where she was and Linda had been able to pacify her, just in time as it turned out because Jimmy was to find out later that she could be pretty difficult especially where her only child was concerned. Linda's comment, "I knew you two would get along well," confirmed Jimmy's suspicions about the whole thing but it turned out to be great night especially when the families got together later and exchanged gifts and hugs. There was no doubt that Jimmy would ask Hazel for a date and of course the go-to person was, who else? Linda, so there was to be no secret romance or even no secret at all, which was not Jimmy's way of doing things. Apparently he did not have a choice, this particular time, but he would in future, he told himself. Jimmy and Hazel met outside the Queen's picture house a couple of weeks later, it was still mid-winter and she had a lovely winter coat on and knee length white boots and really looked a treat as her mam had already told her so before she got the bus to go down to Chester. Jimmy thought the boots looked awful, too big, and Hazel saw at once his glance even though he didn't say a word, but she spoke first,

"what's the marrer wi' me boots then?"

Kind of caught him off guard,

"nothing, there're fine."

"Well what you lookin' like that at them for,"

"holy shit, this is going to be a great night isn't it"? He managed to keep from saying out loud.

"I just thought they looked a bit big that's all," he said.

"Well, me mam made me put them on," Hazel shot back.

Jimmy gave her a hug and told she looked smashing and suggested they get into the place before the big picture started. Amazing what a hug and a few kind words can do isn't it? He was aware of his responsibilities and the fact that Hazel was still at school, probably in her last year, but there was a big difference especially where parents were concerned so he made sure she got on the bus for home and she assured him that the bus stop was seconds away from her house and they arranged to meet again but would see each other at the dance, and that was it for a while.

In fact, Jimmy was already considering that Hazel was too young for him, but he was always thinking about her and had thought, maybe later, when she gets a bit older, we'll get back together but, then again, do you think she is just going to hang around doing diddly squat waiting for you to make up your mind or for her to get a bit older. "Bloody hell", he thought, "women"!

A NOT QUITE A GEORDIE STORY

He loved his job but was struggling a bit and his work mates helped him get through the first year because they seemed to know that he was having some difficulties with certain things, notably his draughting presentation and his printing for example but his big concern was the engineering studies at the college, he knew the college forwarded progress reports and exam results to his boss but it wasn't as if he was missing classes, it was not his attendance, it just seemed at times as if the engineering subjects were beyond his grasp and there was still that one lad, Brown, who seemed to take a delight in making Jimmy's life miserable with his loud comments. Going into the second year, after the whole class had passed the first with flying colors, Brown had made his usual loud mouthed comment to the whole class, that he was surprised to see Blandy again as he never thought he would ever pass. Jimmy had just about had enough, he walked over to him and quietly said, "listen fuck head, if you make one more remark about me or to me, I'll take you outside and pound the fuckin' shit out of you, and I don't care if I get thrown out, do you understand"? Jimmy and Mr. Brown were not exactly best buddies after that but there were no more comments. One of the things that he liked and took advantage of was the relationship and approachability that some of the teachers or lecturers at the college offered, not all of them, but one likeable chap was his mathematics teacher who would continue to be his mathematics teacher throughout the whole five-year engineering course, providing he passed each year. Mr. Thomas was a young chap, not long out of university and maybe because of his age and youthfulness gave Jimmy the confidence to speak candidly about his concerns and difficulties with the syllabus. But Mr. Thomas had no industrial experience whatsoever, that was not the issue, it was just Jimmy's inability to comprehend some of this new theoretical mathematics plus the fact he could not see how this type of mathematics could possibly be of any use in engineering draughting and as the years went by those thoughts continued to plague him, especially as Mr. Thomas, who was without industrial hands-on experience could only provide theoretical problems and solutions.

Going one day a week to Gateshead Tech. was a vastly different experience compared to going full time to Sunderland Art College. For a start the students were different, harder may be the word, and there was not the friendliness nor the after-hours get together or the dances that seemed to be part of the Art College's routine, maybe it was a 'welcome to the real world' wake-up call as some would have said, but working life had become Jimmy's world, as if he had a choice. He was approaching eighteen years old, had been sampling the beer for some time, although still under age, his stomach was beginning to adapt so he wasn't throwing up after every extra pint and even lunchtime at the tech. the boys would head over to the Springfield Hotel for a pie and a pint much to the distaste of whichever lecturer was on class that afternoon. Jimmy was one of the younger members of the' Chester gang', so while the rest of them were all of drinking age and enjoying legal visits to the pub, he was still worried in case he was caught and in particular on the gang's Saturday night visits to the wrestling at St. James's Hall in Newcastle they would chose a pub up in the Haymarket area which had a back door and a view of the front door so that when the Bobbies burst in, which they did without fail, the lads would up and run out the back and they never did get nabbed. They did have a scare one time though when coming back from Newcastle in a newly acquired van driven by one of the few lads with a valid driving licence, as they were coming into Chester, they failed to negotiate a roundabout, in fact nobody even saw the roundabout until they hit it at some speed and careened across to the other side, eventually finding the road again. The bunch of them who were in the back were tossed around like rag dolls but were not seriously hurt and the incident was cause for great entertainment later on. Like the joke going around the table, eventually there were stories of the van turning over and throwing everybody out and ending up in a ditch and they must have been going at one hundred miles an hour and the driver showed amazing skills but really they were just a bunch of lucky sods who didn't kill themselves.

The 'Welding Company' where Jimmy worked had a football team which turned out on Saturday morning, unless they were all working and one of the other apprentices in the office played for them and another one played for his local village team, both teams were of a very high standard as Jimmy noticed from the sidelines, where he watched without bringing attention to himself. But he thought, "if only, I wish," the reality was, he may have the skills but just not the confidence or the physical build to play on those teams, nevertheless he continued to practice his skills and keep up his fitness level just in case an opportunity arose. He still had the occasional game for the cycling club but time seemed to be so short what with homework and other stuff but one thing that his employer made a big issue of was the social side of life and they were always organizing different functions and he would participate as best he could in anything they came up with. One day an announcement was made at work, they were to have a 'Riverboat Shuffle'. "What the heck is a 'Riverboat Shuffle?" Jimmy thought. Anyway, it turns out that these outings were quite popular and groups would rent a boat, complete with live band or just a disc jockey, the boat would be stocked up with booze and the group would embark on an excursion up the Tyne from the quayside to some village up river which, needless to say, had to have at least one pub and after an hour or two in the pub they would return down river to the quayside where the group would staggeringly disembark and find their way home. Jimmy thought what a great night he and Bob could have as they had drifted apart just a little trying to contend with jobs and such and maybe this would be a change from the Monday and Friday night dance routine and the pair of them were now playing darts for a local Chester pub on Tuesday nights. So it happened, Jimmy bought the tickets for the mid-week event and off they went to Newcastle to meet on the quayside with the rest of the group, which they did and they all boarded the boat and this time it would be disc jockey who would be playing the non-stop hits of the day. The first thing they noticed was that there were two nice looking birds dancing together and no evidence of boyfriends around. They both thought it was a bit too early to start chatting them up so they entertained themselves with tossing a few beers back and admiring the sights. The boat ride was reminding Jimmy of years before when during a school outing for educational purposes the class had been taken on an excursion up the Tyne and all he could remember were the smirks from the boys and the giggles from the girls as they pointed out the floating rubber blobs as these things danced passed the boat, talk about being naïve, he had no idea until years later, what they were. Even his sister had assumed he knew a little bit of life when she told him a story of her friend who, with her husband, had been painting their new house and had run out of paint. So the lady had gone to the paint store and had asked for a tin of 'Durex' paint. The man behind the counter said, "okay, I can give you a tin of 'Dulux' paint but if you want 'Durex' you'll need to go to the 'Chemist' next door." The darkness came down and the lights came on and the boat became a hive of activity, the music played and the beer flowed and Jimmy and Bob got those two birds up to dance, everything was hunkydory as they say and suddenly they were at their turnaround spot. The pub they found, had a piano and Bob banged out a few songs while Jimmy tried his best to keep pace with him and then it was time to board the boat and head back. Those two birds seemed more friendly or was it just wishful thinking and imagination but whatever the feeling, Jimmy and Bob rekindled their interests and were never turned down in their dance requests with the two girls and it seemed like maybe this was going to turn out into a really good night even though they were not on home turf. So that's how it went until the boat docked and everyone was saying goodnight and what a great night it had been as they headed down the gangplank and onto the quayside. Jimmy and Bob kind of realized that the two girls had distanced themselves from them in the frenzy of disembarking so they rushed around trying to find them and suddenly there they were on the quayside where they made contact again and started up the usual patter and chatting up. Something was not quite right and then it was obvious when two lads appeared, these were real 'Townies' as Eddie would have referred to them, long draped jackets with velvet collars, drainpipe trousers, thick wedge soles shoes, long sideburns and when they produced the bottles they were carrying, they were not offering drinks and suddenly those two birds were not so attractive any more. Words were spoken, accusations made and denied but then a punch was thrown, no one could remember who threw that first one, and then it was fists and boots and only the sound of a broken bottle brought the fight to a halt with some of the boat's occupants who had remained behind finally coming together, stepping in and preventing what could have been a nasty incident and human nature being what it is, that is how a great night would have been remembered and it would have been a pity. Jimmy was severely brought to task the next day at work for being the cause of the situation despite his innocent protestations and if the truth were known, he was extremely thankful that those people had chosen to stay behind for a little while whatever the reason.

Jimmy had turned eighteen now so there were no more problems like getting chucked out of pubs for being under age but people were still chucked out for fighting. The gang had settled on one particular pub in Chester front street as their local and meeting place, this was 'The Crown' and as there was a 'High Crown' further up the street, 'The Crown' was referred to by all as 'The Middle Crown'. There were many pubs in Chester, so much so that it was a Sunday night favourite for bus trips to descend on Chester and unload their cargo at the bottom of the street. The unloading point just happened to be opposite the Bottom Chapel, much to the Minister's horror and the congregations's dismay and then the bus occupants would embark on various drinking orgies. One of the challenges was to go up and down each side of the street, have a drink in each pub and still be standing at the finish, no mean feat as the Sunday drinking hours were much shorter than the weekly hours. Good for local business could be the argument but the Methodist community certainly did not approve. So it was in the 'Middle Crown' one Monday night around eight o'clock as they were just getting a game of dominoes going before heading off to the dance when they noticed a chap, (actually they figured it was a cop) talking earnestly with Stan the owner/manager. After a while the chap left and Stan beckoned Jimmy over to the bar and told him the gist of the conversation which was basically that the coppers in the station, which was just across the road, were staging an identity parade. Apparently there had been some breaking and entering going on over the weekend in and around town with somebody getting roughed up a bit and the police had a suspect in for questioning. The police were pretty sure they had the right guy but needed some more evidence and were hoping that the suspect would be picked out in the line-up. Jimmy said to Stan, "Why me?' to which Stan replied, "because you look a bit like the suspect." Even the thought of getting paid some cash just for standing in a line with some other guys had Jimmy wondering whether this was a good idea, especially if there was a chance he may be picked out by mistake, anyway, curiosity got the better of him and off he went to the cop shop. There were a few instructions from the detective in charge of things like, stand perfectly still, look straight ahead and DO NOT make eye contact, and remember we are sure we have the person responsible. "Yeah but," thought Jimmy. There were about a dozen in the line and the victim was going down the line from Jimmy's right to left and have you ever tried not to make eye contact when a person is standing directly in front of you, his face about a foot away from your face and he is staring intently at you? Of course Jimmy would swear later that the guy doing the looking spent twice as long looking at him than he did anyone else. The gang all had a laugh when they heard the story and were still laughing when they got to the dance and Jimmy had such a tale to tell Hazel when he saw her. Jimmy and Hazel were an 'item' now, as they say, and they spent a lot of time together especially at weekends, as there was not that much free time for them during the week. They did not have much money, Hazel had a factory job which meant working shifts and Jimmy was on apprentice wages but they enjoyed each other's company and visited one another's house often where both sets of parents got on really well with each other. Their houses were about three miles apart on a regular bus route, actually the bus route that Jimmy had taken to Sunderland Art College, which seemed a long time ago to him. In fact, on the few occasions where he had walked home from her house, the walk took him down Newbridge Bank where he and his dad had gone fishing so many times and his dad had regaled him with the Lambton Worm and other stories. Jimmy had wanted to grow up, but not that fast!

Time was indeed moving fast for Jimmy Bland, his mam always said that as you get older, time goes more quickly and she appeared to be right again. Late 1961, Jimmy and Bob decided to go to a dance

A NOT QUITE A GEORDIE STORY

at Pelton Fell on Saturday night. Hazel was away somewhere and Bob's girlfriend was with some friends, so off they went, took the bus up. They were not really looking for anything, just out to enjoy the music, both were quite content with their present circumstances and girl-friends but a change of scenery may do them good, they thought. The dance was pretty much without incident, Jimmy knew a few of the lads from his school days but nobody was looking for trouble, the only incident was when he was warned off for no apparent reason by some lad he vaguely remembered from his school days and as the dance ended late and the buses were no longer running the pair of them had to walk home, about two miles, no big deal. They had just rounded the corner onto the Chester road when they were stopped by a police patrol car with a uniformed sergeant and constable in it. Apparently someone had kicked in the front window of the local Co-op store which was located just a few doors down from the dance hall and two figures had been seen running from the scene, so the police were asking for witness statements and any other information which may be helpful. The lads did not find the two cops very friendly, more intimidating than they needed to be and in fact there were some insinuations if not downright accusations but Bob and Jimmy kept their cool and answered the questions, after all, they had nothing to hide or to fear. After a while the two uniforms got back in their car and continued their patrol while the lads plodded on down the hill towards Chester discussing all kind of important things, as youngsters do at that age. They were nearing the bottom of the bank where the Chester and Pelton Fell roads intersect and were just approaching the bridge over the Cong Burn when the patrol car approached them again, coming from the direction they had been walking. There was no delay and no warning, the doors flew open and orders were shouted for them to stop. Jimmy, by this time was getting a little bit tired and ratty and said to Bob, "just keep walking, they've already spoken to us and they know that we had nothing to do with any store window, anyway they have our names and addresses," but Bob said, "we'd better stop, I don't like the tone of their voices." Bob stopped and was immediately collared by the sergeant while the younger constable took off, shouting, "hey you Bland," and grabbed

Jimmy, kind of bear hugging him and wrestling him onto the bridge where he held him against the stone parapet. To say that Jimmy got the shock of his life would be an understatement, but more was to come as the constable started to let fly with his fists and every blow was accompanied by a torrent of curses and name calling. Fortunately Jimmy had winter clothing on and the blows were aimed at his upper body where he was able to parry a lot of them but even so there was some force behind them and it was relentless. At one stage he heard Bob asking the sergeant to stop the onslaught but there was obviously no response as it continued and Jimmy started to weaken but he knew he dare not go down as he was certain that this moron would put the boots to him and he dare not throw a punch of his own even in self-defence. It was the torrent of bad language that was being spewed forth that amazed him, "you effin' this and you effin' that," followed by, " I'm going to knock that fuckin' chip off your fuckin' shoulder you fuckin' little twat, or do you want to go over the bridge you fuckin' little piece of shit," and Jimmy actually felt himself been lifted slightly and he thought to himself, "copper or not, there is no way I am going to just let this ape throw me over the bridge." Then it all stopped, the patrol car drove away, Jimmy and Bob just stood and looked at each other. "What just happened?" and neither could remember what, if anything had been said to them at the conclusion of their most unpleasant experience to date, but it was to have a lifelong effect on Jimmy Bland.

    The pair of them met the next day as they had made arrangements to go to the pictures on the Sunday night and they discussed the previous night's nightmare. Of course, when Jimmy had got home the night before, his mam was still awake and she immediately said, "what's happened?" Jimmy's pale face and mother's intuition were instant giveaways and he told her the story. "Well, you must have done something," was Lizzie's response, which was expected as the police were above reproach as far as she was concerned. Anyway Bob and Jimmy decided to report the incident and would do so late that afternoon as they had to pass the cop shop on the way to the pictures. Who do you report a police incident to? – The police? They had to make do with describing the two policemen as they had not thought to take note of numbers, it's all very well afterwards for people to say, "you should have got their badge numbers," but it's a different story to do it at the time. It was a simple matter to check who was on duty in that area at that time and so the powers that be knew at once who the lads were talking about but they did not let on and after their statements were made they were assured and comforted by the knowledge that the two in question would be severely dealt with. Yeah, right! The incident did not affect Jimmy's daily routine although mentally it was to haunt him for a long time after but Bob experienced some problems. His work as a driver of the grocery truck for the Co-op took him all over the Chester area but more importantly it took him around the Pelton Fell area and within days of the incident he ran afoul of the constable again. Bob was a good driver but the threats were repeated again and again for him to watch out because the police did not take kindly to being reported, and sooner or later Bob was going to suffer so he had better watch his back. Word filtered down through the grapevine that the two rogue cops had been spoken to about the incident but that was as far as the wrist slapping went. Did anybody figure any different?

CHAPTER 8

Still Learning the Hard Way

How strange it is when relationships evolve without apparent control or direction but then again maybe it is because there is no attempt to control circumstances that suddenly there appears a situation that just seems to happen. Not that Jimmy and Hazel's relationship was not wanted, it was just a case of how did it happen without either of them directing traffic, so to speak. Any decision now to reverse the direction of flow would be catastrophic or so it might seem if either of them ever stopped to think about it. But neither of them had any reason to stop and take stock of the situation, that's not to say there were no concerns or problems, like the Saturday night he was over at Hazel's house and planning to stay over when her mam and dad got out their collection of Embassy coupons, these were coupons that were included in packets of Embassy cigarettes and a certain number collected meant a gift or merchandise could be acquired. Well, it was kind of late, Jimmy had been hoping that Hazel's parents would toddle off to bed and leave the two of them alone for a while but apparently it was not to be and he was expected to join in the counting of these coupons. There were literally hundreds of the things and he started off with the best intentions but he suddenly threw his fistful of coupons all over the floor and said, "what the hell am I doing counting this crap, bugger this". Not one for mincing words, Hazel's mam said, "there's the door, get out and don't come back until you learn some manners". It was well after midnight,

A NOT QUITE A GEORDIE STORY

Jimmy grabbed his coat and stormed out of the house, "fuckin' hell," he said to himself, "Saturday night, my promise has gone right out of the window and now I've got to walk home, why can't I keep my big mouth shut?" The following Sunday lunch time he went down to the pub and got pissed which, as everybody knows, just makes things worse. There had been one or two incidents leading up to the one on that Saturday night which kind of had Jimmy wondering if the direction he was heading was the one he wanted to take. He was still young and Hazel was even younger, there was no doubt they were a good match and were continually being complimented when they appeared together but these niggly incidents were bothering him. He decided he would cool it for a while and started going out with a girl from work, she was from the Gateshead area and had an older brother who had assumed the role of his sister's keeper. Well, it's all very well being protective of your younger sister but there is a limit to the intrusion or invasion of privacy, or so Jimmy thought. It got so bad that when Jimmy and Brenda announced they were going to a late movie one night he tut-tutted like an old hen and was voicing his concerns when Jimmy just blurted out, "look, do you want to come with us, maybe you can sit between us but I'm bloody well sure I'm not paying for you as well." Then he finished off with, "Jesus Christ, I do not believe this." Which kind of started a bit of a row but in the end Jimmy and Brenda went to the movies as planned. Brenda was a lovely girl, a bit more than what Jimmy had bargained for in as much she was her own boss, she knew where she was going in life and there were some serious conversations but all the while he was wondering how Hazel was and maybe he should make the effort to go up to the shop where she now worked. She had given up the factory job and he had seen the difference straight away because her outgoing and pleasant personality made her presence behind the counter such a delight for customers. His mind was wandering again and he figured he had better make up his mind what he wanted but what brought matters to a head was the Saturday he had arranged to take Brenda to a show in Sunderland. After having lunch and spending the afternoon together they caught the early bus around five o'clock at the bottom of Chester and proceeded up the street, there was another stop at the top of the street beside the Black Horse pub and who should get on the bus, but Hazel, who had just finished work at the newsagents and she just glared at the two of them. Of course Brenda did not know Hazel but she knew of her and the whole episode was most uncomfortable although nothing was said. Obviously the night was spoilt, the mood just fizzled out like a damp firework and Brenda wanted know where she stood in the overall scheme of things because his reaction at seeing Hazel could only mean one thing and that meant that Jimmy and Brenda were finished. He should have made the decision to go up and see Hazel ages ago rather than have some sort of incident bring things back into focus and there goes that need again to control your own circumstances and not to have decisions made for you because of inaction or procrastination.

The first thing Jimmy had to do on the road to mending bridges was apologize to Hazel's mam and dad, which he did along with presenting them with some flowers. Then he had to win back Hazel all over again, or so it seemed as she had not been idle either, having picked up with an old flame going back to her school days. They had a favourite pub, up around the 'Hairpin Bend', as everyone referred to it so Jimmy suggested they have a nice early meal at a quiet restaurant then down to the pub for an hour or two. Sounded like a plan, the restaurant was nothing fancy but within his budget and they made it to the pub around seven thirty where they found a couple of seats in the back room and settled in to watch some locals playing darts. People were coming and going and then Jimmy was aware that there was a group who seemed familiar to him, at least the guys he thought he knew. Eventually they all got together and figured out who was who and why the faces were familiar and mostly it was school and Chester dances that were the common thread. In no time at all it was closing time, the bell was sounding and last orders were being announced and when Jimmy said they were leaving to get the bus they were offered a ride home. What the heck, it would be a bit cramped but they would manage, they had not gone far when someone suggested a ride down to the coast seeing as it was nice night. "Drink's in, wit's out," as Jimmy's mam would have said, but off they went. "Only one thing," the driver said," I need petrol and I've no money, in any case all the petrol stations are closed no.," "No problem," said his mate, "I'll show you a place where I used to work." It was indeed a petrol station and garage and it was closed but this lad proceeded to do something at the pump, got the thing to work and filled up the car. "Let's get out of here," he said. Jimmy could not believe what was happening, they had just broken into a garage and stolen gallons of petrol! Hazel was busy gabbing away with the girls and not showing any interest in what was going on outside but Jimmy wanted out, except he did not know how to go about it and then they were speeding down towards the coast, all the time getting farther and farther away from home. He had not had a lot to drink and was suddenly very sober at that point but he needed to go to the bathroom, he figured at the speed they were going they would be at the coast in record time or worse, they would be pulled over or worse still, end up in hospital. Why did he let this happen? "When I should open my mouth, I don't," he thought. They made it to the coast in one piece, Seaburn, Jimmy figured, so at the first opportunity he found somewhere to pee, "I know this area," he thought, "there should be some steps down to the beach about here." He found the steps alright, in the darkness he went straight down them and landed in a heap on the sand below, fortunately the tide was out. Staggering back up to the top, Hazel asked him what happened because he was there, then suddenly he wasn't, so he just said he missed a couple of steps. The group started wandering along the street, gazing in the windows of the few shops, all closed and barred obviously and probably with wired security especially this one jeweler that the driver and his mate had suddenly taken an unhealthy interest in. Jimmy began to get an awful feeling especially when he espied one of them searching around for something to throw through the window. "You had better open your mouth now dummy, and make it good or this night is going to turn into an absolute disaster," he said to himself. The driver's mate was getting ready to launch a building brick through the window as Jimmy gently took hold of his arm and hoping that the feeling of panic welling up inside him did not reflect in his voice, began to explain why it was not such a good idea to throw the brick. He pointed out that the stuff on display was hardly worth anything, the better stuff would be inside, the windows were reinforced glass and the metal bars would never give way and he pointed to the security cameras (actually Jimmy figured there were none), saying that even now all of them would probably be on tape and at the instant the brick struck, alarms would sound and how do you suppose we would all get away? An eternity seemed to pass but for whatever reason the driver's mate threw the brick away and said, "let's go home, I'm sick of this place." Jimmy grabbed Hazel and almost ran back to the car, he was in a cold sweat and it wasn't until they were on the road heading back to Chester he realized that his leg hurt and he could feel something warm trickling down into his sock. "Bloody hell," he thought, "I've gone and pissed meself." Closer examination told him that not only was his leg bleeding but the pant leg of his new suit was torn and Hazel, who was sitting on his lap started to question what all the squirming about was for. "I'll tell you later, when we get home," he said, and to himself, "if we ever get home." But home they did get, more by good luck than good management and over a cup of tea before bed they discussed the evening and Jimmy realized that Hazel was unaware that the night had been so close to disaster. One of the few occasions that he was thankful for the chatter boxes that women can sometimes be, and he certainly wasn't going to enlighten her, ignorance is bliss, or so it was in this case, but, for him, it was another lesson learned and he was not going to forget it. It's not that he was a perfectly law abiding citizen by any means, he had intentionally trespassed, ran from the police and had even stolen a pipe from Woolworths on a dare from the lads, (he had gift wrapped the pipe and given it to his dad as a birthday present) but what had just happened was completely different in the sense that it was criminal intent and subject to jail time and all because he didn't go with his initial instincts which asked him just how well he knew the people and more to the point he had not considered his responsibility to Hazel. This was a scare and a worry which he shared with no-one.

Far from winning Hazel back in the manner that he had planned, he had to come up with some other strategy and the opportunity came when the some of the drawing office staff, the less- older ones it needed to be said, began talking about and organizing a night at one of Newcastle's night clubs. Hazel was still under drinking age but she would be well looked after once she was inside the place so Jimmy put their names forward along with some cash because you don't get into these places for nothing. The night club chosen was the Club-a-Go-Go, Jimmy had never heard of it but he was not into the Newcastle night club scene and he was glad to see a couple of the people going were ones that he had formed a special friendship with and he knew Hazel would immediately take to Alan and Alma. Alan worked directly across the aisle from Jimmy and everything about him was professional and yet to see him come in to work on a morning wearing his leathers and motor cycle helmet he looked like a rough and tough biker. He, along with another workmate rode identical red BSA 500cc Road Rockets which were powerful bikes by any standard, yet Alan would strip off his outer wear and underneath was his suit and immaculate white shirt and tie. He would roll his shirt sleeves up a certain way to make each arm identical with the number of folds and his attention the whole day was devoted to his chosen task. There was a lot to be learnt from Alan because he had already passed his final examinations and was considered a senior draughtsman who was willing to pass on any advice. The evening had great promise and Jimmy was determined to stay sober and stay close to Hazel because he knew her parents had not been too thrilled about her going to a night club, especially in Newcastle so this was his big chance to make amends. Jimmy and Hazel went to Newcastle by bus but they had made arrangements with Alan and Alma to get a ride home, a bit out of their way for them so it was certainly much appreciated and Jimmy had no concerns this time that they would indeed be taken straight home. What a night it was, it was a relatively small group who eventually went to the night club but everyone knew everyone else and it was a pretty much top notch night club which attracted some well-known names and to Jimmy's surprise and more so later on in life when he realized the headliner that night was the Alan Price Set, of course starring Alan Price who would go on to make quite a name for himself but in the band at that time was Eric Burdon who later became famous as Eric Burdon and the Animals.

Although Jimmy was determined to stay sober he was feeling no pain as the night wore on and so comfortable with his friends and even when Alan said, "Haway ower here Hazel and sit on me knee and we'll talk about the first thing that comes up," he still laughed out loud along with the rest of the crowd but he knew if it had been anybody else but Alan there would have been hell on. He also knew that Hazel looked ever so good with her short skirt and splendid looking legs and she had been getting some admiring glances, more the reason for him to keep control of things.

That night went a long way to make amends for his past behavior and got him back into the good books, not just with Hazel and her parents but with his own parents who had sensed some uneasiness and were becoming just a little concerned, it may have been the company he was keeping or the drinking and smoking and all night card games but they knew Hazel had a way of keeping him in check so they were delighted for the two of them to get back together. The next opportunity came a month or so later when another Riverboat Shuffle was being arranged as the previous one had been such a resounding success. When Jimmy's name appeared on the sign-on sheet there were a few comments and he was asked to control his behavior but he assured everyone there would be no problems this time as he was taking his girl-friend. The night of the event came around quickly and off they went to Newcastle again, meeting down on the quayside as usual, different boat this time but same routine, although there were more traditional jazz or Dixieland tunes, which were great to dance to. Hazel was a good dancer, whereas Jimmy just plodded along, trying to look as if he knew what he was doing and they were bopping or jiving as it was known in some circles. There was only room for two or three couples to do this type of dancing on the small boat so there was some good fun in trying to get the floor and it was on the way back down river when Jimmy and Hazel were on the floor with another couple that the girl accidentally trod on the top of Hazel's foot. Normally this type of mishap would have been no big deal but the girl was wearing stiletto heels and the damage was seen immediately as the foot began to swell and change colour but even at that time Jimmy did not think it was too serious, so they sat out the rest of trip and it was only when Hazel rose to get off the boat that she realized she could not put any weight on the damaged foot. Jimmy ended up carrying Hazel up to the bus stop and when they got back to Chester he carried her home and explained the situation to her mam and dad. It was a week-night but John said he would take Hazel to the hospital next morning as he had a car and Jimmy should stop by the house next evening to check. Hazel was in quite a bit of pain and ended up missing work a whole week which did not sit well with anybody, especially her mam who made no bones about the fact that accident or not, Jimmy should have somehow prevented it. Two forward and three back Jimmy thought, story of my life, can't win for losing.

As the year wore on, Jimmy was nineteen and was really maturing, although he never stopped to think about stuff like that, he just wondered when his next football game was and would he even get picked because he was not making a lot of training sessions. The Monday and Friday night dances were still a priority and he didn't mind when Hazel danced with her girl-friends because, after all, the girls could dance. Strange how you never saw two lads dancing together, both probably would want to lead although Jimmy didn't think that was the reason at all. What he did know was that he would be taking Hazel home even if she did have the occasional dance with some guy who figured he had a chance. He was into his third year at college in the September after having passed both previous years and his third year, if he passed would give him an engineering certificate and the opportunity to progress in a slightly different direction. He had always realized the significance and importance of study although he had not always been too willing to make the right choices but now, after having achieved more than he could ever have imagined (and more that some would have thought possible) he was willing to make sacrifices. He was working with lads and men who came from much tougher backgrounds than him who had seized opportunities and come out on top because of sacrifices and hard work.

About this time there had been an important change in his company and this had been in the form of a take-over, his company had been bought out and merged with a much bigger organization and although this had no immediate impact on anybody there were a series of announcements, one of which heralded the fact that there were to be a number of additions to the drawing office staff. Around about this time Jimmy had been completing some of his factory floor training and was quite enjoying the difference, not to mention he was wearing coveralls and getting dirty and also taking a lot of ribbing from the workers on the shop floor as they always seemed to class the office staff as snobs and nose in the air types and made good natured fun of anybody that came down for training. So it was then that Jimmy was called back up into the office to meet and work with a technical writer who had come up from the head office in London as the merger had brought additional lines of equipment for the factory to manufacture and the company felt that there was need for instruction manuals and spare parts lists where there had been none or where the old ones needed to be updated and Jimmy's job would be to work with the new technical writer and prepare drawings for these manuals without neglecting his other work and studies of course. "Stick a broom up my arse and I'll sweep the floor as well", thought Jimmy but this type of work is what he had always wanted to do and he was good at it and he relished the opportunity although he felt that this London technical writer was not too impressed with his skills and would have preferred to bring along his London based colleagues. He was disappointed that the boss did not give him a different place to work because there were times where he would have to strip down a gearbox for example and lay out the parts to enable him to identify and draw them and this was all done at his draughting desk. "What a fuckin' mess", he thought one Monday morning when he walked in after a none too pleasant week-end and an upsetting row with Hazel and to top of it all a new estimating format had been introduced, after all it was an engineering company and this format entailed requiring more detailed and identification of small parts, even down to the nuts and bolts to comply with the new company's programme and this format had to be incorporated into the detail drawing so every little thing had a common identifying number. Well, what with the additional work which Jimmy had now to contend with plus this new stuff, his mind wasn't really into this new format of identifying individual bloody nuts and bolts but unfortunately for him, his compliance, like everyone else's, was being monitored and a tally was being recorded down in the estimating department where the importance and success of the project was key. He did not know, but was soon to find out, that he was getting a real bad reputation for not being accurate with the new process and he was called into Mr. Dryden's office to account for his mistakes. The office still stunk of roll your own cigarettes but maybe it wasn't quite as bad as usual, "has the little guy been trying to stop"? wondered Jimmy, but that was as far as his musings went as Mr. Dryden just laid into him. "What's got up his nose," he thought and then the light came on. It was to do with the new numbering procedure and the estimating department had finally had a belly-full of Jimmy's mistakes and decided to report him to his boss. Well, he had never been one for just standing and taking it, whether it was punches or a tongue lashing and he started arguing the toss, which was a complete no-no under the circumstances and he blurted out, "It's not my job to put numbers against things just to make it easier for the estimating department, my job is to make drawings.". There was a distinct silence as Mr. Dryden got up, stepped out from behind his desk and drawing himself up to his full height of five-feet nothing said, "Your job is to do whatever I tell you to do and if you have a problem with that then the sooner we part company the better, now get out 'til I decide what to do with you." Jimmy knew he had overstepped the mark again and would be very fortunate to come out of this incident with his job intact and he had so much going for him. Oh Boy, he was sweating buckets and shaking like a leaf as he made his way to his desk with quite a few eyes on him because the dressing-down had been heard through the closed office door by just about everybody. It was one of the worst moments of his life and there was nowhere to hide and nobody to talk to because he was completely and utterly wrong and totally out of line.

 The following day was his one day per week release from work to go to college and it was just as well there were no exams that day because he would have failed the lot of them, such was his state of mind. He had no sooner clocked in the next morning at work when he was called into the manager's office, he had just got to his desk and was adjusting his drawing board equipment when he heard the dreaded tap-tap tapping of little feet and then a voice which in no way matched the frame from which it emanated, "Bland, in here now." "Holy fuck," Jimmy thought, "and a very good morning to you too Mr. Dryden." The manager proceeded to tell Jimmy that he had spent part of yesterday looking at the damning reports from the estimating department and while there were a number of errors in the new numbering system attributed to Jimmy's lack of care and could have been avoided, the bulk of the problems were with material take-off from drawing information which allowed for cutting and machining and scrap and if not done correctly resulted in underestimating and job losses. In the manager's opinion it suggested a lack of engineering experience on Jimmy's part in that area and he was prepared to be lenient providing some conditions were met. The conditions were additional training and a stint in the estimating department where his work would be monitored and an apology to all involved for causing a disruption to an otherwise pleasant working environment. Jimmy nearly fell over backwards with relief when it all sunk in and he most profoundly expressed his gratitude and thanks to Mr. Dryden. (later, when he thought of his grovelling performance he wondered why his knees had not been showing through his trousers and his lips were not sore). But he had learned his lesson and vowed that he would not jeopardize his career again whatever the circumstance and that Hazel had to be his overriding priority.

September came around too early as usual and this was an especially important college year for Jimmy as the examination come the following June was for his Ordinary National Certificate in Mechanical Engineering and a first time pass would give him other options, maybe a full time diploma course leading to a degree. Heady thoughts indeed but first things first and he knew he was certainly not a shoo-in to succeed but he knew what had to be done. Things between him and Hazel were good, better than they had ever been in fact and it was Jimmy who had changed although there was never any discussion but as far as Hazel was concerned there was never going to be anyone else now in her life. So the weeks drifted on and suddenly his workmates were talking about the Christmas Dance, making sure that the date was kept free of other events. The venue was The Old Assembly Rooms in Newcastle, a very prestigious place and although there probably would be no dinner jackets and ballroom gowns, a certain respectable attire would have to be worn and there definitely would be no throwing up on the carpets or the dance floor as was frequently the case at the Chester dances. Jimmy was really looking forward to it and the opportunity to show off Hazel again, he had really worked hard since the college year had started again in September and now he figured he deserved a nice Christmas break and one or two parties thrown in for good measure. Jimmy always felt comfortable with Alan and Alma, in fact he thought the world of both of them and often over the course of the evening at the Christmas Dance they would all be together, either dancing with each other's partners or just sitting having drinks in the lounge and it was during one of these occasions when he and Alma were alone that somehow the conversation had got around to the importance of relationships and how was it with Jimmy and Hazel. Women just seem to be able to do this flawlessly without batting an eyelid and suddenly the unsuspecting person blurts out, "what do you mean?' knowing full well what was meant. He realized that it was time for him to start thinking seriously about Hazel but Alma had certainly caught him off guard with her comments and questions and then Alma ended the conversation with, "you should marry Hazel you know." He was still sitting there with his mouth open when Alan and Hazel came off the dance floor.

 Many years later Jimmy and Hazel, along with their two boys would travel from their home in Canada and pay a surprise visit to Alan and Alma. It took them a couple of days and some phone calls but eventually they tracked them down and it was wonderful reunion.

 The year 1963 broke with the traditional New Year's Eve parties and tickets were obtained for the Chester Dance which turned out to be the opposite of the company Christmas Dance at the Old Assembly Rooms as far as music, drinking, people spewing up all over the place and Jimmy and Hazel were glad to leave early and go with the rest of the gang around the houses which was another tradition where toasts were proposed and when the magic countdown to midnight arrived there was much singing and celebrating and cries of, "All the best for the New Year." Jimmy loved this scene and he vowed he would carry on the tradition wherever he went, even the 'first foot' which was the first person across the threshold of a home after midnight and this person, if he carried the correct objects would dictate the future good fortune for the year for that home. Then it was back to the daily grind for most and Jimmy had not forgotten the promises he had made to himself to really make the effort to get through this important college year. But what continually came into his mind were those words of Alma, "you should marry Hazel you know", he could just not get the words out of his thoughts and for all he knew, Alan and Alma may have put a few words in Hazel's ear that night, so what was Hazel thinking right now? Anyhow the priority was the June examination coming up and although it would be tough he had every confidence especially when Mr. Thomas, his maths lecturer, seemed to be providing him with some additional tutoring and advice. Jimmy had his twentieth birthday in April and the thought that he was no longer a spotty faced teenager gave him nightmares sometimes, especially when he still had a pale spotty face. He really sacrificed a lot of free time to do extra study so he was as prepared as ever he could be when the examination time came around and then it was a question of waiting and because this examination was assessed externally the wait was even longer than usual. The long-awaited results came out, oh no! he had failed Maths but passed the other subjects and he was absolutely distraught. His first thoughts were to throw in the towel and forget the whole thing but there were commitments at work and a contract signed was a legal contract. When the time came around he enrolled at the college to take the full third year course again because the whole course and all subjects had to be re-taken, not just the failed subject and it took him a while to come to grips with the situation especially the lost opportunities. But after a while he stepped back was able to view the situation better and realise he needed to look at his achievements and not missed opportunities and devote the same effort as before to go forward. What he really needed to do was open up and discuss things with someone but he had always found that difficult, preferring to soldier on by himself, making his own decisions as usual. Then he started remembering some of Alma's advice and realised the very person he should be opening up to was Hazel and it dawned on him that because she was younger in age he had been treating her not as an equal and not deserving of making important decisions. Hazel herself seemed to be quite content to let Jimmy make the decisions and more or less was fine with everything that was going on but he was determined to change all that and would renew their relationship and tell her he loved her. Suddenly it was out, even if all of the thoughts were just in his head, he had admitted to himself what he had known for some time but had been too full of his own problems to acknowledge the fact.

At work, everybody was sympathetic about his failure to obtain his ONC but they all reminded him it was not the end of the world and he was not the first one to fail an exam and he certainly wouldn't be the last and just to keep up the effort and he would get results. The good natured ribbing he used to get for his Durham accent had decreased but started up again just to make him laugh and become his normal self again. Even Mr. Dryden offered some advice and told him not to worry about his job or anything like that, he was doing fine and after a bit of a rocky start with the new Technical Writer there were now some good reports and his work looked great when it was put together and bound professionally in a company manual. This certainly put his mind at ease, for a while anyway and he relayed this information to Hazel who had responded to his renewed attention and change of attitude with silent thanks and some expectation that maybe there was something else coming. Indeed there was something else coming and Jimmy popped the question soon after and there was never ever any doubt in Hazel's mind what her answer would be, a resounding yes and tears all around, but he brought her down to Earth again with, "I suppose we'll have to get a ring." "How romantic", she thought, but that was him all over and she would not have expected anything different. They had a little get together with their parents and eventually word got around to all their friends, "no going back now," thought Jimmy at one stage.

That was the setting then as September rolled around again and off he went to college, going to be interesting to see who passed and who failed thought Jimmy as he found his classroom and wandered in. A good number had passed and one or two had apparently decided that three years was enough and decided not to continue but there were still a few returning familiar faces and greetings were exchanged. The first lesson that morning as it turned out was Maths and in walked Mr. Thomas, the same Mr. Thomas from the year before and he was as interested as anybody to see who was returning and he spotted Jimmy straight off. He said, "of all the people I thought may fail my class, I never thought you'd be one of them". "Some consolation that", thought Jimmy but when asked what had happened, he had no answer and of course he had asked himself that same question over and over again with the same response. The thing that was bothering Jimmy was the fact that he knew he was going to spend more time working on the failed subject but what if he failed one of the other subjects? He must not let them slide and what if he failed Maths again? "Shit," he thought, "I could go on forever second guessing and worrying, got to get those thoughts out of my head." And that is exactly what he did, his priorities became work and Hazel but he still allowed himself one night out per week, usually Friday, to meet with the lads for darts and dominoes and that's where he was on November 22 1963 when the news came through that Kennedy had been assassinated. What a tremendous shock to everyone and it became one of those unfortunate events that whenever it is brought up in conversation everyone can remember where they were at that very time. Bob had been absent from the pub for a few nights but he was in that night and he was talking to Jimmy at the bar when he apologized for his breath and said that he had had all his teeth out and had new ones put straight back in the holes and was feeling a bit under the weather. He had not told anyone of his intentions and caught them all off guard but of course Jimmy was full of questions, having come close to using that procedure a couple of years before. After Bob's description he was glad he had gone the more traditional route. The other topic of conversation that night was that two of the gang had got into a fight after the dance the previous week-end and had been arrested and charged with weapons offences because of the broken glass in their pockets which happened durng the fight. Of course the glasses had been stolen previously from the pub and this taking of glasses and ashtrays from pubs had become a bit of a hobby for all of them especially when out with their girlfriends as the girls had handbags sufficiently large enough to hide such things. This event reminded Jimmy of the party at Fred's one Saturday night where he had taken a couple of bottles of Newcastle Brown Ale and put one in each pocket of his overcoat which he hung on the post at the bottom of the stairs. Before he had a chance to retrieve the bottles someone knocked the coat off the post, breaking the bottles in the pockets. Jimmy had been furious and demanded that Fred pay to have the coat cleaned which resulted in Fred almost been prosecuted because he had not made the cleaning company aware that there was glass in the pockets. Really the coat should just have been thrown out as the pockets were ruined anyway.

The lads had been meeting like this on the same nights, sitting in the same chairs, drinking the same make of beer for some considerable time and discussions more often than not got around to the future. Somebody remarked that two years from now or five years or ten years they would all still be sat there and in fact there were one or two older regulars in the pub who may as well have been cardboard cut-outs, they had been sitting in the same spot for so long. This had got Jimmy thinking and he and Bob would often continue the conversation during the walk home and both decided that maybe they should start thinking more seriously about their futures. But still, by the time Christmas came knocking he was thankful for a little holiday which just amounted to those few days between Christmas Day and New Year's Day but were most welcome. To start things off on the right foot the drawing office had their regular Christmas Party, not to be confused with the Company Christmas Party or Dance. On Christmas Eve at noon the Drawing Office shut down production and the booze came out, this had been paid for by subscriptions over the previous weeks and carefully hidden away and food was also laid out, party trays put together by the canteen ladies who were also invited to partake of the refreshment. There was music and paper hats and stuff and other office departments were welcome, even the estimating department joined in and all previous animosity was forgotten. By mid-afternoon most people were feeling no pain and some were having to arrange for a ride home, such was their condition. Jimmy was okay, he was catching the bus as his bicycle was put away for the Winter but there was one draughtsman, a tall ex-guardsman, Harry was his name, who Jimmy knew quite well and liked, Harry had told him one time that during his stint in the army he had actually done the Buckingham Palace guard duty thing where he wore one of those huge Busby helmets. In fact, there had been another do where the two of them had shared a ride home at some un-godly hour and instead of going straight home they decided to go ten-pin bowling where neither of them could barely stand up, never mind keep score. Needless to say, they were thrown out of the place. Anyhow Harry was in a slightly inebriated condition and Mr. Dryden offered to give him a ride home which he gratefully accepted and that was the last that was seen of them that afternoon. It wasn't until everybody returned after the Christmas break that the story got out that Harry had thrown up all over the boss's car, hadn't been able to call out a warning, just opened the window and let fly. There was laughter all around the drawing office but not when Mr. Dryden was in earshot that's for sure. It was the same Harry who later on had a real unfortunate accident with his portable circular saw and this was no laughing matter. Apparently he had been working on a project at home, as everyone does, using his power saw to cut some wood, nothing wrong with that fact except it would be considered extremely foolhardy to be wearing carpet slippers when doing so. Who will ever know what preoccupied his mind for a split second, enough for him to lose concentration or was it simply a knot in the wood, but whatever the reason he lost his three biggest toes on one foot and they ended up in his sock, in his slipper. Harry was quite a guy, not a softy by any stretch of the imagination plus he had a terrific sense of humour, which some may have considered weird but he returned to work after a spell and people gathered around his workplace to help in any way and to just wish him well on his return. He chatted for a while with everybody then proceeded to take out a matchbox from his pocket, he kind of did it of nonchalantly and was still chatting as he slid the matchbox drawer open and inside, nestled on a bed of red stained cotton wool was his big toe. No kidding, there were some who nearly fainted right on the spot! Then the joke was discovered, it was his thumb protruding through a hole in the bottom of the matchbox but it was the way Harry did it, no one suspected and everyone was caught by surprise. When things quietened down a bit somebody suggested he play the trick on Flo, one of the canteen girls, or whoever was on duty that morning when the morning tea and coffee was brought up. It turned out to be Flo and she was one of the younger and better looking 'Molly on the trolley' girls as they were called and she was always good fun. The problem was she almost fainted and had to be caught before she fell and although everyone laughed about it later, including Flo, it was time to put that joke to one side just in case.

Jimmy was twenty-one years old on the fifth of April 1964 and because he and Hazel were saving like mad, putting every spare penny away they did not have anything spectacular planned for his big occasion but they did go out for a few drinks with another good friend, Chris, whose wife Cathy was expecting their first child but had opted to stay home. They were not out too late and came back to Jimmy's parent's place for a snack when there was knock at the front door and it was Cathy's mam with the message the Chris had better come quick as his wife had started. In a flash Chris was gone and suddenly the night was empty but the next day they found out that Cathy had a baby girl before midnight so she was indeed born on Jimmy's twenty first. His twenty first birthday also brought him another wage increase and the company had provided him with decent increases over the years, some were automatic increases, some were merit increases and his work was being appreciated more and more by management. He was even given small projects to complete from start to finish and it was a bonus for him to see his work being assembled on the shop floor from his own drawings. The June examination came far too quickly for him, although he could not possibly have prepared better he was worried sick, he wasn't sure if he was going to get another year of day release from his company and if he didn't then it would mean three evenings per week at the college which was a daunting thought. Jimmy was determined to continue and obtain his Higher National Certificate in Mechanical Engineering which would mean a further two years of study even if he passed the June 1964 exam, but he and Hazel had discussed tentative dates for getting married and the year they had decided on was 1966 and he knew if his studies were not complete by then it would be difficult, if not well-nigh impossible for him to complete after getting married.

Jimmy had even given up his football just so he could spend more time with his studies and one of his favourite quiet places was down in Lambton Park on a Sunday morning especially if he had spent the previous night at Hazel's with her parents who both worked for Lord Lambton and their house was rent free on the vast Lambton Estate. He had found a beautiful little spot not far from Hazel's house where he would unload his book filled haversack and get to work, safe in the knowledge that he would not be disturbed, except for this one memorable Sunday morning. He was spread out on a small grassy hill with a bit of a vehicle track running around the side of it when out of nowhere an Estate vehicle appeared, or at least it had the appearance of being an official Estate vehicle, it stopped and out stepped an official looking gamekeeper. He wore a tweed jacket with leather elbow patches and trouser bottoms tucked into his wellies[12] together with a cloth cap on his head and no doubt, thought Jimmy, he had a game dog hiding nearby just waiting for the master's command, "here Trixie, kill!" He had seen this type of person before, full of their own importance, oblivious to any form of manners, with the 'I'm in charge' look and obviously intending to show any trespassing poachers how he dealt with them. No doubt running to Lord Lambton at the first opportunity, grovelling at his feet and informing him of his capture and requesting permission to have the scumbag peasant locked in the dungeon. Before Jimmy had a chance to open his mouth and wish the good fellow a very good morning he was met with a, "do you know you are trespassing on private land?

---

[12] Wellies – rubber boots known as Wellingtons

I've a good mind to call the police and let them take care of you," and on and on the gamey gabbled, almost frothing at the mouth. Jimmy thought at one stage that maybe the gamey was upset because his regular favourite sheep had turned him down and he had had to make do with sleeping with his wife for a change but it was only a passing thought and he managed to get a word in with his explanation that he was studying for examinations and was obviously not setting traps or otherwise killing the wild life and was not intruding on anyone's space. But his explanation went unheeded and the gamey's response was, "how would you like it if Lord Lambton came parading through your house, through your living room uninvited?" Jimmy thought, "this fuck-head is mental, he's probably got a double-barreled twelve gauge shot gun in the car so I'd best keep my mouth shut". The incident ended with the gamekeeper demanding that Jimmy pack up his stuff and he would be escorted to the Estate boundary where he would be off-loaded on the understanding that he would not return. So that is what happened, but the gamey drove his car right past Hazel's house to the Chester bus stop at which point Jimmy immediately turned around and walked slowly back in the direction they had just come but then turned and went into Hazel's house. He knew the gamey was watching and it took all of his strength to stop himself from turning around and saluting him with the finger but he also knew that Hazel's dad would be getting an earful the next day because he was going to tell John the whole story. Sure enough, when they were all through dinner, which actually turned out to be pheasant from the Lambton estate, Jimmy had seen the bird hanging behind the yard door the day before, he told Hazel and her parents what had happened that morning. John just laughed and said, "oh that Skeggy is just a blow hard, he was just trying to do his job, why did you not just tell him who you were?" It had never occurred to Jimmy to try to explain that he was engaged to be married to John's daughter, he had stayed at John's the previous evening as he had done lots of times and had visited friends on the Estate many times. No, Jimmy preferred to see the real Skeggy, if that was his name.

As the pair of them were saving up for their wedding most of their weekends were spent at one or the other parent's houses and when Jimmy was at Hazel's all four of them usually went to the bingo in Sunderland, sometimes they ventured into Newcastle but Sunderland was much closer. Jimmy absolutely detested the mindless game of bingo and refused to play, which did not sit well with the company he was with as was evidenced by the looks on their faces but he compromised and bought his share of bingo cards but after a few 'houses' he would pass his cards over to Hazel or her mam for them to play. The part of the evening he did enjoy was the card games the four of them held before the actual bingo started, as the place was so popular, people had to be there an hour early just to get a seat or get the car parked. So it was a case of grin and bear it at the bingo as it was with the Embassy cigarette coupons which he now helped count just to keep the peace. Before he knew it, the day of the examination dawned and he didn't even open his books that morning as he figured if he didn't know his stuff now, he never would. He didn't exactly sail through the exam but it turned out to be one of the few occasions where he finished the paper with time to spare and he used that time to just go over one or two answers. He felt good heading back home on the bus but he knew the danger of being too smug so he kept his thoughts to himself and did not commit to any comment with anyone. The results came out around the end of July and he was informed by mail with the letter stating that he had been successful and that an Ordinary Certificate in Mechanical Engineering would be forwarded to him in due course. No fanfare, no attaboy but he knew the effort that had been required to obtain the certificate and was quite chuffed as people were prone to say in those parts and it was fair to say his parents were delighted and told him so.

It was then a case of enjoying what was left of the summer, he was still learning to drive and in any case buying a car, even a banger, was totally out of the question but he and Hazel managed some day trips away as they had planned their summer holidays to coincide and that year they had arranged to visit Linda and her husband for a few days in Bristol. Even after he had finished secondary school, Jimmy had continued writing to car companies and aircraft manufacturers for photographs and specifications of automobiles and aircraft but with his new skill as a Technical Illustrator and the training he was obtaining at the 'Welding Company' he had actually enquired about a job at The British Aircraft Corporation in Bristol and had received an invitation to attend an interview, so he and Hazel used their stay at Linda's to coincide with his interview. Jimmy was trying to stop smoking and at the time of the Bristol visit had been stopped all of six months, no mean feat but he had stopped for six months before and had started again so it was a challenge and unfortunately Hazel had got into the smoking habit and Jimmy was convinced he was the cause of it. Both Linda and her husband smoked so it was odds on that Jimmy was going to start again but he held on or held out as the case may be and went to his interview with his portfolio of drawings tucked under his arm. He was suitably impressed with the treatment he received, more like he was overawed by the experience, he was given an expense chitty for meals and another for travelling expenses and the interview was very informal where he was given the opportunity to display his work and he felt very much at ease, remembering the time at school when that interview was just the opposite. Coming out of the interview and not far from the company gate was a pub and without realising the time he went in for a pint, of course it was three o'clock and they were closing but he was allowed a pint, he felt he could do with a lot more, maybe he was fortunate they were closing. He needed to collect his thoughts and try and remember where he was supposed to be meeting Linda and her husband who were picking him up. The pint was finished in record time, helped by the fact the bar staff were cleaning up all around him, looking at him and then looking at their watches so he got the message and wandered out in the general direction he figured he should be headed. He thought he was in the right place but hoped they would show up soon as he had actually no idea where he was but noticed a small newsagent's shop on the corner and he suddenly, really, wanted a cigarette. He bought a packet of Players Gold Leaf and a box of matches and they remained unopened in his pocket for the longest time, if only his ride had arrived, but it didn't so he opened the packet and lit a cigarette. He felt dizzy and as sick as a dog, so bad in fact he had to have another and he knew it was game over, he had lost again and then his ride arrived and he was busy answering question after question. They got back to Linda's and she had prepared a meal and they relaxed with a few drinks, talking about everything and nothing, it was so good to be all together again even for just a short while so that when bedtime came around Linda just said there's your room, pointing it out to Jimmy and Hazel, see you both in the morning and left them to it. There was no discussion, just acceptance of the fact that they were going to sleep together and this mini holiday was going to be remembered as something special thanks to Linda. Jimmy had known Linda since they were both four years old, they were born in the same year and their birthdays were just three months apart and there were no secrets between them, never had been but Linda seemed to have this uncanny knack of knowing stuff, especially where Jimmy was concerned, a bit unsettling at times, he thought, but other than Hazel there was no woman he thought more of than 'our Linda'.

CHAPTER 9

Time to Move On

Friday nights in the Middle Crown usually and eventually came around to conversations regarding the future, their future, the North East's future, England's future, the World's future – pretty serious stuff for a night out with the boys but Jimmy and Bob still continued those discussions as they walked home and Bob had said at one stage he was thinking about going to Australia. England had for some time been offering, for ten pounds, a one-way ticket to Australia as an immigration incentive. Some pals from Jimmy's neighbourhood had already taken advantage of the offer but when you are young and single there are no limits to your options are there? These are phases that every young person goes through but that fact doesn't make it any easier for the individual does it? Any thoughts that Jimmy may have had that he was now a Senior Draughtsman at twenty-one years of age were quickly dashed when he brought up the subject at work one time as he was smartly informed that at twenty-five years old he may be considered senior or he may not, depends. But something was bugging him, maybe it was a case of the grass being greener on the other side, but he was certainly unsettled, was it because he had started to realise that he may be capable of something different, something more than he had thought possible or was he just a dreamer? Was it something Bob had said recently about thoughts of going to Australia? Whatever he was thinking of or dreaming of had better take a back seat because he now had responsibilities and commitments and one of them was Hazel, she was the most important, and the other was college and finishing his engineering course so he could provide Hazel with a good life through him having a good job. Life doesn't have to be all work and no play but it has to be worked at, there's an oxymoron if ever there was one, but they found a way to spend time with each other and save money on weekends by baby-sitting at some friend's house or looking after pets while the owners were away, stuff like that but there was one friend's kid, actually a real good friend of Hazel's parents, who had asthma really bad and Jimmy hated being there because the poor lad had some real nightmarish episodes which Jimmy at times didn't think he could cope with and sadly, just a few short years later he was to learn that the boy had died from his affliction.

September again brought on another college term and this was the first year of the Higher National Certificate course in Mechanical Engineering that he was struggling through, a pretty worthwhile achievement by anyone's standards. Lots of theory, lots of formulas, lots of calculations but as usual lots of help and encouragement from his workmates but the onus was on himself to spend the time learning, which he did. There must have been an unconscious decision by Jimmy to apply himself to the task of passing the college examinations and to make whatever necessary sacrifices were required to achieve that goal because when the results came out the following July he passed, not with flying colours as they say but with sufficiently high marks to be proud of and to earn some attaboys from his boss. But still the restlessness nagged away at him and he had learned from his past experience that it was better to discuss things with Hazel and he wanted to do that, she was so much a part of his future that he could not even visualise life without her but he knew she did not feel the same restlessness he did and would the fact that she was an only child be an issue if he decided a better life for them may be had elsewhere. He then realised that was the problem, he felt he needed to get out of Chester, needn't go too far, he thought, so that visiting would not be a problem but why leave a secure job? His boss had told him after passing the first year Higher National course that there would always be a job for him at the 'Welding Company' and with the take-over a while back by a large corporation there was the possibility of a transfer to London if he wanted to pursue that option. The correct and logical choice would have been to stay put for a couple of years and then take stock of the situation but Jimmy was not known for always making correct and logical choices.

Then he saw an advertisement in the paper for a Mechanical Engineering Draughtsman and he just knew he had to apply for the job. The intriguing part was the company that was advertising was the very same company he had recently finished a project for, the fact that this company was thirty-five miles away and he had no transport never even entered his head. Jimmy had, under supervision, completed all the drawings for a piece of equipment which would facilitate the welding of large pressure vessels of the type used in the oil and gas process industry. It was a big company and he had no idea if the advertised job was even in the same division or location but he did recognise the contact address as being the same as that on the project documents. The other thing that never entered his head immediately was the fact that he and Hazel had decided on a wedding date and this was to be the following year in September, nevertheless he forged ahead with his job application. He had some serious thinking to do and decisions to be made as he figured if he got the job, he had less than three months before the college year started in September, three months in which to find digs in a new town, enroll in a new technical college for his final year, come to some agreement with Hazel, after all they were engaged to be married, and try to finalize some wedding arrangements rather than leave everything to Hazel, and look for a house: all that and starting a new job!

Hazel's dad, John, was a great help, he was the only one with a car but he offered time and again to accommodate their requests and when Jimmy received word about the job application, John immediately offered to take Jimmy (and of course Hazel) to the interview. He had been involved in numerous interviews since leaving school and never ceased to be amazed at the excellent treatment received at these events and this one was no exception. Not exactly wined and dined but immediately put at ease by being allowed to discuss his work and his involvement and completion in the recent mutual project which seemed to create some interest and the promise of reimbursed expenses which is always a plus. The company may have been looking for someone more senior but were very interested to hear about his desire to complete his Higher National Course and said that if he were to be successful in the interview he would be given assistance in enrolling at the local college and assistance at finding acceptable digs if it was his wish to relocate. Jimmy felt great with his presentation and was very optimistic about his chances but he knew the higher he went the bigger the fall. He obviously had created some sort of impression because a week later he was offered the job and by signing the enclosed contract he would be accepting terms of service and what amounted to, an increased salary. He was over the moon but at the same time very apprehensive and scared shitless as he admitted to himself when he got the news, but, as he had figured many times before, once the decision was made, there was no turning back.

    He came to rely on John more and more and when he thought back later he had to admit that some things would not have been possible without John's help and much later when he realised how much he owed his and Hazel's parents and then suddenly it was too late to say thank you. The Bland family always shared a chuckle when they talked about the 'Man from the Pru' coming around to the house on Saturday mornings. Saturday mornings were quite busy with the paper boy, the council rent man, the 'Man from the Pru,' and the tea man form Rington's Tea all looking for money. The only one that was not looking for money was the local constable who always seemed to want know where Jimmy had been the night before, sometimes Jimmy wanted to know where he had been the night before. Also every second Saturday Uncle Bill would stop by for a chat and a cup of tea before taking Eddie to Newcastle United's home game. It was through Bill that Eddie decided to buy a season ticket but when they took Jimmy to the match they all stood on the terraces. Bill's accent had more of a pronounced 'Geordie' sound to it, possibly because his job as a salesman took him to a lot of Newcastle area stores and Jimmy would pick up on a lot of his words and how they were pronounced and then at the football match he was surrounded by real 'Geordies'. But he loved every minute of it especially when the crowd suddenly burst into a rendition of 'The Blaydon Races'. "Simply amazing how they all seemed to start singing together without a leader," thought Jimmy. When Lizzie realised and accepted the fact that Jimmy and Hazel were serious about their relationship and had actually announced their engagement, she confided in Jimmy that, years before, on the recommendation of the Prudential Insurance Company, she had taken out additional insurance for him on the understanding that when the time came for him to purchase a mortgage for a house, this insurance, if payments were up to date, would almost guarantee him approval. This was excellent and completely unexpected good news for Jimmy and Hazel so off they went with this new information in search of some suitable accommodation. The location of his new job was Stockton – on - Tees and they found a small new housing development just outside the village of Norton, just north of Stockton. There were some foundations started but all they had were the building plans and brochures and the promise that the houses would be ready by the following September, everything fitted in with their timetable and the village of Norton was absolutely beautiful. So they put in their offer, no mean task as they had to beg and borrow sufficient money for a down payment and off Jimmy went to the Prudential's head office in Durham with his mam's policy carefully in his grasp. After waiting for what seemed a ridiculous length of time he got to see somebody and was informed quite bluntly that obviously there had been some misunderstanding as the granting of a mortgage was simply based on the applicant's income and his income was far below that required for the house he was interested in buying. The prudential rep. may as well have said, "everybody knows that, dummy," because that is what it sounded like. Jimmy was gobsmacked, all he could think of was his mam, paying into this rubbish all these years, thinking she was doing such a great thing, all that money which could have gone towards something more important. He was absolutely incensed and he called the Prudential Insurance Company a bunch of thieving bastards and if the man from 'The Pru' ever came to his mam's house again he would personally beat the snot out of him, he was so upset he could not remember later how he got to the bus station.

Maybe Jimmy was admired and complimented for his decision making by a lot of people or maybe there were some who were just shaking their heads, in actual fact he was one of the head shakers himself and was constantly questioning his own motives and reasoning. Nonetheless there was no reversal and his plans went ahead. First of all, he managed to get enrolled in the local technical college for his last year of the engineering course, three nights per week, six-thirty pm until nine pm; this is going to kill me, he thought at one stage and then he arranged digs at a place just off Yarm Street about a twenty minute walk from the college and about a thirty minute walk to his new work place. Once all those arrangements were made he turned his attention to his leaving the 'Welding Company'. His last day had already been finalised and any back pay or holiday pay due had been agreed upon so all that remained was the dreaded last day when all his work mates had agreed to give him a good sending off at the local pub. He never, ever forgot that day. The people that showed up for a drink or two whom he hardly knew, the bosses from other departments, lads from off the shop floor but his workmates from the office, who stayed until just about closing time, made him realise just what he was leaving and giving up. When all the best wishes and hand shaking ended and the last friend had left, he was on his own, surrounded by empty chairs, empty bottles, empty glasses and an awful empty feeling in his stomach and he felt so down and alone.

This was a period in his life which was hectic, stressful, with unanswered questions and doubts about his ability and decision making. If he had stopped for a while to think about others and their feelings, he may have demonstrated more thoughtfulness but, as is often the case, he realised much later how Eddie and Lizzie must have felt, their pride for him making progress in the working world, the upcoming marriage but all counterbalanced by the fact that he was leaving home and as Joan had already been left home a few years, this was a particularly sad time for his parents. They hid their feelings well but alone at night, things may have been a little different.

A NOT QUITE A GEORDIE STORY

The timing was so tight between leaving the 'Welding Company' and starting his new place of work that he was only able to manage a few days to make last minute arrangements and then the dreaded Sunday night came when he boarded the bus for Stockton with a carry-all for the week ahead in digs and some work instruments and books that he thought he may need.

He caught an early bus to Stockton that first night just to give himself time to get his bearings and to get organized but even so he did not get to meet the other lodgers until the following night. He did meet the family of the house, there was Ted and Jean, the owners of the home and parents of son Ian, who was about seventeen years old and nephew Ray, a bit older. The house was a reasonably sized terrace house with a small back yard which opened out into a laneway which gave access for the 'bin-men'[13] whereas the front of the house opened out on to the street with only a footpath separating the pedestrians from the traffic. "It does not look big enough to house all of us," thought Jimmy with that first impression which is usually right, "but I guess I will find out soon enough." Somehow Jean had managed to accommodate her family plus three other lodgers besides Jimmy, and he found out the next night that the three other lodgers were Glaswegians employed by a company working on the oil rigs down at the docks on the River Tees in Middlesbrough. The three men became firm friends of Jimmy's, each one looking out for his well-being, always making themselves available with help or advice and occasionally offering to show him some of the lesser known or less desirable places of interest along Stockton's High Street or riverside. (As part of his education, they told him)

Jean had set times for evening meals but seldom was there a full complement for them. Jimmy was okay most nights, finishing work at five o'clock, he could get his dinner eaten, then head off to night class at the college for six-thirty until nine-thirty on Monday, Tuesday and Thursday and with Wednesday night off he had time to do homework and sometimes even get out for a while but the Glasgow guys, Joe, Frank and Hughie, worked overtime most nights

---

[13] 'bin-men' – North Eastern term for garbage collectors

and would arrive back at the digs at different times to find their dinners in the oven. Jimmy was finding it ever so tough going, not only were the final college year subjects difficult but his new job was challenging to say the least. The location of the new job was indeed the same as where his recent engineering project had been installed and in due time he managed see it in action. When he hesitantly asked questions on the shop floor as to the equipment's operation and performance he was chuffed to be told it did everything it was supposed to do, and well. He even got to see some of his drawings scattered about the shop floor but it wasn't in him to start shouting, "those are my drawings!" Maybe the workers were just using them to wipe the grease of their hands. In reality he was assigned to a department where he felt like a fish out of water, he learned fast though and managed to accomplish the tasks he was given but after a few weeks he was moved to a different location in the plant, a smaller engineering department specializing in process equipment for the oil and gas industry and other fuel systems equipment. Jimmy was more at ease in this new environment, plus it was closer to his digs but he longed for Friday nights to come so he could get off home to see Hazel.

There were opportunities to talk with Joe, Frank and Hughie but very seldom was there an opportunity for all of them to sit and chat together. Joe was more senior both in age and experience and seemed to have more free time, so Jimmy and he would share family and work interests and other good stuff. In time Jimmy looked to Joe as something of a father figure. One thing he had noticed since moving to the Teesside area was the acceptance of his accent, not actually acceptance as such, but nobody seemed to give a shit how certain words were pronounced. Of course this could be location, location, not too far from Wearside with Teesside being right on the border with North Yorkshire and such a diversity of dialects right there on the riverside. He knew Joe and the boys were making very good money and although Jimmy had received a wage increase upon moving he looked at his pay stub occasionally and wondered, "what if?" At one stage he was feeling a bit down, probably feeling sorry for himself, if the truth was known and he had said to Joe, "I wish I could get a job with you down on the rigs." Joe did not reply immediately but seemed to choose his words carefully as if he realised that Jimmy was maybe feeling a bit homesick and missing his girl. He explained that yes, they did make good money but it was tough, hard and dirty work with long hours and most of the men were away from home with bills to pay and mouths to feed with a good portion of their wages going back home to pay for these commitments. He went on to say that he,

Frank and Hughie had talked amongst themselves and were happy for Jimmy and a little bit envious because they had seen the potential for a great future for him once he got his engineering certificates and gained a bit more experience. In fact, Joe added, they were going to make doubly sure that Jimmy stayed the course and achieved his best possible results as long he remained part of their household family. Jimmy was overwhelmed and a little choked up with this admission of friendship and realised again that people are not always to be judged by their appearance or tough talk but need to be assessed individually with an open mind.

Although the college night classes were a tough slog he did make a couple of friends in the class and one was to remain a good friend for the rest of his life. Steve worked at the same company as Jimmy and had been there a number of years and this was his second attempt at passing the Higher National Certificate course final year, so he was able give Jimmy some valuable tips, but Steve was a quite a character, a bit of a comedian and an excellent caricaturist and the pair of them would sit in the back row of the class, tell jokes and laugh at Steve's doodles. This was a good outlet for Jimmy, a means of relaxing but he knew he could not afford to fail the final examinations because his wedding day was fast approaching and although he had good intentions of continuing his education after his marriage he secretly admitted to himself that that was probably not going to happen. But the pair of them managed to find time, usually Wednesday nights, to get out and have a few pints, although Steve had to put his foot down a couple of times as he told Jimmy, "all you want to do is fight after you've had a few!" and then there was the time when they went to the local night club where Jerry Allison and his make believe band 'The

Crickets' were playing one night and Jimmy got so pissed he couldn't find his way out of the place, Steve just left him to find his own way home and really laid into him the next day at work.

    The days turned into weeks and life at the digs was pleasant enough, though a little crowded when everybody was there but the meals were good and Jean was really a smashing landlady, as for husband Ted, Jimmy couldn't figure out whether he worked, either full time, part time or no time but that never seemed to bother anybody. Jimmy would spend most weekends back in Chester usually over at Hazel's and get the late bus back into Stockton on Sunday nights. Stockton, late at night, was not a place for the faint hearted, especially on weekends and one Sunday night as Jimmy turned off the High Street to walk up Yarm Lane, people were still milling about after the pubs had closed and a fight broke out outside one of them as he was passing. He had seen fights, been in a couple himself but had never seen two girls go at it like the two that night. He could not take his eyes off them, not for one minute, it looked like they were determined to kill each other and inflict as much damage as possible while doing it, not to mention the language that was being used. In no time at all, quite a crowd had gathered, some male pricks were actually egging the girls on but fortunately the police arrived and it was toss up to see which would arrive first, the Paddy Wagon or the Ambulance, they actually arrived together. Another Sunday night he arrived back at the digs, where Jean was waiting for him to ask if he would mind sharing his bedroom (which meant his bed) temporarily with another worker who had been left stranded with no place to go. Ritchie was his name and he was a tall, rough looking customer but friendly enough and he came in later that night when Jimmy had already gone to bed. It's not the best of occasions when the first time you meet somebody they hop into your bed, "might have been different if it had been a woman," thought Jimmy, he was so tired that night but found it really difficult getting to sleep, didn't know which way to turn. Ritchie was up and out before Jimmy got up the next morning and that evening he was determined to get some more details from Jean as to how long Ritchie was going to stay, she had no idea actually, she said. Jimmy thought, "well, this is a fine how-do-you-do isn't it. Have I just got to grin a bare it?" he didn't think much about that comment until later. As it happened Ritchie turned out to be not such a bad guy but on the fourth night of his appearance at the digs, he didn't show, either for dinner or at lights out, none of the other lads had seen him either. Not much anybody could do about it, Ritchie was an adult and obviously quite capable of looking after himself, he also worked on the oil rigs down at the docks, but the next night the police showed up looking for him. Apparently he was wanted in connection with an incident in a pub a couple of streets away where a customer had been bottled and was probably going to lose his eye and the description given for his attacker certainly fitted Ritchie, so he was now on the run. Nobody that Jimmy knew had any idea what happened to him after that.

On one of the few weekends that Jimmy managed get some overtime he stayed over in the digs in Stockton and Joe, Frank and Hughie proposed to take him out on the Saturday night and introduce him to the 'Dolly Sisters'. He was a little apprehensive to say the least as the time approached for them to hit the street, he had dressed casual with jeans and thick shirt but he noticed that Joe was wearing a suit and tie, Joe was always the gentleman, the others were more casually dressed. There are some real dives in Stockton especially off the High Street where they enjoyed a couple of pints and then Joe said let's go to the 'Black something or other', Jimmy never could or did remember the name of that place but there he was introduced to the 'Dolly Sisters'. In their presence he felt so awkward because these girls were so good looking and sexy, they really made a fuss of him and the Glasgow lads laughed and laughed at his apparent discomfort, but really he was enjoying every minute and was turned on, not just a little either. He knew the lads were making fun of him but after a while he went along in the spirit of things and then Joe said, "ask them how much they cost". Well, Jimmy didn't know if Joe was kidding or not so he said to the one that was showing him the most interest, "Joe says to ask how much," thinking he was being smart in phrasing it like that, but this was the most important night of the week for these working girls and he suddenly realised he may be treading on thin ice. Then Joe stepped in to lighten the situation by saying, "the lady charges a packet of cigarettes, surely you've got that Jimmy?" Then he knew they were all in on the act so it all ended with drinks all around and a good laugh and another education lesson for Jimmy. These occasional educational sorties are okay he thought at one time but he must not let them get to be a habit or become any sort of routine, which he didn't, but even so there was another time, a Wednesday night it was, where he had knuckled down to some serious study as there were mid-term tests coming up. He now had a smaller bed in a smaller bedroom as there had been some switching around in the digs and he was getting kind of weary as the time wore on, so as he was thinking of calling it a night there was a knock on his door and it was Frank trying to whisper quietly, but in a voice likely to wake the dead, "hey Jimmy, can I come in, you want to help me celebrate?" And in rolled Frank with a half full, not half empty (there is a difference when you don't really want any) bottle of whisky. "Shit," thought Jimmy, "I'll never get up in the morning." The he said, "okay Frank I'll have one only while you tell me what we are celebrating." Jimmy had heard a while back from the other lads that Frank had got done one night for being drunk and disorderly in Stockton High Street, and apparently today, this particular Wednesday had been his day in court. Nor really having any money, because he was pissing it away as fast as he was making it, he had decided to represent himself. The charges were read out and the judge had asked for clarification a couple of times because the arresting officer had decided not to show up and the clerk of the court was having some difficulty reading the charge sheet and statement and then Frank was asked to give an account of his actions that night. Well, the long and the short of the story is that the judge sympathized with the arresting officer and acknowledged that the officer could have misunderstood Frank's incoherency by the fact that Frank was an Irishman from Scotland living in England, (Teesside actually), most of his teeth were missing and his accent was such that it was really difficult to grasp or interpret his words. So Frank was acquitted and he was celebrating and that was why he was in Jimmy's room that particular Wednesday night. And that was why

A NOT QUITE A GEORDIE STORY

Jimmy was late for work the next morning with a thick head and a tongue just as thick.

The building of Jimmy and Hazel's new house in Norton was progressing really slowly and he was at the building site as often as he could manage but what was he to do or say, except complain to the builder which obviously became a waste of time. He eventually accepted the probability that the house was not going to be ready for them to move into right after their wedding in September. On his next weekend visit home, he gave Hazel the disappointing news and they discussed their options, which were not many, but the outcome was they decided to find some suitable temporary rented accommodation in Stockton which would take them over the coming winter into the following spring where they had been promised the house would be complete. With this additional task in his head he took the late bus back to Stockton on the Sunday night and arrived at the front door of his digs to find Jean waiting for him with some devastating news – husband Ted had died of a heart attack the previous day. Jimmy did not know what to say, the other lodgers had all found temporary digs and had offered to help Jean in any way they could, but Jean's concern was for Jimmy that night, even though she must have had a great deal else on her mind. She gave him an address to go to in the next street where arrangements had been made for him to stay for the next week or so. Off he went with great apprehension because he had heard stories about this particular street, Hartington Road was the name of the street and he found the number he had been given. Hartington Road had, in the past, been one of the posh streets in Stockton, all huge terraced houses but again, no front garden and only a slightly bigger back yard than his present digs, but present day saw these houses in a somewhat different light, some were small businesses, a lot were simply run down but he wasn't complaining, just thankful he had a place to go to and he thought, "this is a big place," as he rang the front door bell. A lady answered the door, he introduced himself, then realised he had been expected as the lady said, "hi, Jimmy, nice to meet you, we've heard a lot about you, I'm Jean's friend Rhoda, this is my place, so come on in and meet the girls." Jimmy thought, "girls, what girls, what a fucking night this is turning out to be." And girls he did meet, a whole bevy of them and as with the 'Dolly Sisters', all very good looking and all very sexy and all on the game. The girls worked the streets, didn't bring customers back to Hartington Road of course, as some of them shared small flats or apartments elsewhere to do their business. They took to Jimmy immediately as he was passed around from one to another, sitting on this girl's knee and then another girl's lap and he found these girls just adorable and so friendly although he was embarrassed by some of the things they said. He thought, "I don't know if a can stand a week of this but at least I will die happy." Then he thought of Hazel and her likely reaction if he told her, so he decided not to tell her anything because maybe she wouldn't believe that nothing ever happened. Did he wish something had happened? He often tossed around different scenarios in his head but he did tell Steve about the experience who just laughed and laughed and said, "are you sure nothing happened?"

Jimmy decided to stay clear of his regular digs for that week, he wanted to help Jean somehow but figured he may just be in the way, after all, he wasn't family and hadn't even known them very long. He often wondered if he was just making excuses and by staying away, would that make life even more uncomfortable when he eventually returned. On top of all that he really was very inexperienced in those types of situations and didn't know how he was supposed to act or what to say. Excuses, excuses he thought to himself, "I wish Joe was here so I could talk to him," but Joe was in Scotland at that time, he found out later.

He missed his football, missed watching Newcastle one week and Sunderland the next and he missed playing the odd game himself. Middlesbrough was now the local club but his interest was not the same even though 'The Boro' had a huge following. His pal Steve was not interested much in sports so there was no common ground there but they played a lot of darts when they could find the time and they were always competitive, playing for pints being a major incentive to win games. Jimmy's dad Eddie, was a season ticket holder at Newcastle, had been for years and had taken little Jimmy to the Saturday afternoon games many times but Eddie was finding the cost of the tickets a little too much as the years went by and was continually threatening to give it all up. It was a long time before he did though. Hazel would complain sometimes if Jimmy went to the game on Saturday when they had so precious little time to spend together now that he was working and living away but he reminded her that he didn't complain when he had to sit through a Saturday night of boring bingo games with her and her Mam and Dad (and no chance of any nooky when they got home he could have added). There was not a lot of time for anything, it seemed, and what little time there was, seemed to be flying by. Christmas came and went, they both enjoyed a few days off between Christmas and New Year and there were family celebrations and get-togethers just as there always had been, so much to be thankful for as they reminded themselves. Jimmy's twenty third birthday was coming up in April and Hazel's twentieth in July of that year and England were in the World Cup and for years after he would tell the story of how he had told Hazel, "if England win the World Cup, we'll get married," and then he would finish telling the story by saying, "and you know what, the buggers went and won it!" The year 1966 was certainly a year to be remembered, so much happening, a new life ahead of them with new experiences and challenges to be met and there had been more than one comment of, "they look so young," but they were up for it and the support from their families never wavered. By the time Hazel's birthday came around Jimmy had already been informed that he had passed his final examinations, his boss had put him forward for a raise and things were more or less back to normal at the digs. Joe and Frank were still there but Hughie had gone for work elsewhere and his spot had not yet been filled in the house.

Jimmy had always thought of himself as a good draughtsman, which he was, but when he saw some of the drawings being completed by fellow draughtsmen in the new company he knew he had a long way to go especially when Steve told him one day, "your printing looks like a fly crawled all over your paper, it's fucking awful." Steve showed him some of his drawings and they were like works of art and really Jimmy was not surprised as he had seen some of Steve's sketches and scripted comments, so he realised he had work to do in that department. (Many years and a lot of drawings later, he was to think back to those early days when draughting was a profession and a skill and he could recognize other peoples' work just by their printing. Then along came computers and Computer Aided Draughting and out of the window went individual recognizable work and of course, by that time, the Apprentice Draughtsman title had ceased to exist along with the five-year apprenticeship requirement programme, and it seemed that anyone could call themselves a draughtsperson as long as they could operate a computer and knew how to muddle through some drawing programme. Such is progress he thought). So he worked at being a better draughtsman but did not find much opportunity to exercise his newly acquired engineering achievements and credentials too much, work experience seemed to be the key words and there was only one way to get that but he knew that in the meantime he had to impress his employer with his work ethic, manner and his knowledge but he still had an eye for the women, especially Joyce, one of the twins who worked in the cafeteria, but he found that she had been tipped off by some well-meaning friend that he was already engaged to be married. "Just as well thought Jimmy, but she is nice and I hope she continues to give me free second helpings at lunch time."

So the days passed into the summer months and he found himself with a bit more time during the week now that college was finished and he and Steve had more pub and night club visits and it was a good period in his life as Steve had also passed his final year examinations. Jimmy thought that despite Steve's apparent lack of interest and respect for college and work and life in general, he really was a smart guy and put on this outer show, but underneath, the real Steve was a much more interesting and likeable person. Jimmy wanted Steve to be his best man at his wedding but Steve wanted nothing to do with that, giving all sorts or reasons, some of which made sense, some didn't, but he accepted his decision and he knew that suggestions had already been made back home, everyone is entitled to their opinion, thought Jimmy but it is my wedding. The fact that he was only home at weekends didn't help either as a lot of discussions and decisions had already been made by the time he was contacted. Nonetheless arrangements continued to be finalized and September tenth moved ominously closer and England had won the World Cup so Jimmy had no out, a promise is a promise, but he had no second thoughts, the England thing was just a joke and he really was 'as happy as a pig in shit' as they used to say in some parts, and honestly he was glad that a lot of arrangements were being made without him being directly involved because sometimes he just felt overwhelmed. "All these people just farting around making silly comments and acting like little girls," he often thought, but he wanted it done right for Hazel's sake so he made sure that the two of them had as much time together as they could manage. Some of the arrangements being made at that time, he found out later, were that relatives from out of town were being billeted at his mam and dad's house and he was going to have to bed down at a neighbour's when he did come home, but he knew nothing of that. The Glasgow lads and Jean really made a fuss of him that last week in the digs and he knew that he was going to miss all of them. They gave him small gifts and a really good old fashioned send-off on the Thursday night at a pub in Stockton and on the Friday he left work early to catch the bus home because there were plans for another 'Bachelor Party' or 'Stag Night' or whatever it is called and Jimmy wondered if he would be up to it having had a good drink the previous night. He needn't have worried.

    It had been agreed that Hazel's cousin Keith would be his best man and this was fine as Keith was a big lad, a darts player and he liked his football and beer, not necessarily in that order and Bob had agreed to be groomsman. Some of the relatives were interested in going out for a drink and there were one or two of Jimmy's mates there who also were keen so they asked him where he would like to go. He had always liked the pub up at the' Hairpin Bend' so off they went and it was a great night especially for Jimmy as he did not have to spend a penny and someone had been charged with the task of getting him home, preferably in one piece. But when last orders were called, and it was really late enough, Jimmy was just getting into his stride and wanted more. The most saner and sober of the group, especially his relatives, tried to persuade him to go home but he was having none of it and wanted to go to the night club at the bottom of Chester and that is where they ended up, not the numbers that had been in the original party but about four or five diehards. Now, unfortunately the night club required membership cards or at least a substantial cover charge to be paid by all and this was a deterrent for all but Jimmy, who had espied a charity group dressed up in white nightshirt type cloaks and nightcaps and with hand held bells ringing were running up and down the street, each one holding on to the shirt tail of the one in front as they went into different pubs or trying to collar just about anybody who might donate a bob or two. Jimmy shouted, "let's tag on to this lot," and before anybody could argue he had latched on to the shirt tail of the last guy and was running up the stairs to the entrance of the night club. Well, most of his party had caught on, fortunately, to what he was about especially Greg, another of Hazel's cousins, who Jimmy just adored and up the stairs they went, straight through the open door and Jimmy found a spot in a dark corner where he figured he would just take stock of the situation before finding his way to the bar. But alas, it was not to be, as if he honestly thought he could get away with something like that, he had no sooner sat down when a huge monstrosity of a 'bouncer' appeared before him and said simply, "OUT." Jimmy mumbled something like, "I'm with them," pointing to the charity group, who all thought that this was great entertainment, but that didn't wash either and now Jimmy was becoming aggressive and looking for a fight. Just then Keith shows up, who obviously knew the 'bouncer' and was explaining that it was Jimmy's bachelor night, he was getting married tomorrow and all that stuff. Well, Jimmy felt that this approach was demeaning and demanded that Keith take on this 'bouncer' and if he didn't sort him out, he would. It never occurred to Jimmy that at that particular moment in time he could have been blown over by a gust of wind, never mind taking swings at a person who was employed to deal with incidents just like that. In fact, he did know all that, he actually knew the bouncer who had trained and ran the boxing classes at the Miners' Welfare', where he had learned the basic skills from the bouncer's dad. But 'drink's in and wit's out' as his mam used to say and while Jimmy was bobbing and weaving and shouting, "come on then, let's 'ave yer," the rest of the lads just sort of picked him up and carried him outside. That, more or less, was the end of his bachelor night, except that after Keith dropped him off at home and he found out that he had to sleep at a neighbour's house, he paraded up and down outside his mam and dad's house yelling, "it's my bloody weddin' tomorra an' ah canna even sleep in me own bed". This went on for a while until somebody opened a bedroom window and shouted, "if you bloody-well divn't get to bed right now Jimmy Bland, there'll be nea bloody weddin' tomorra".

EPILOGUE

But a wedding there was and it was a day to remember even though Jimmy had a couple of pints on the morning of the wedding, on the advice of the neighbor where he had stayed the night before, who told him, "you need a bit of the hair of the dog, that'll put you right." Whether it did or not, no one will ever know. But what he did know and thought about occasionally, was that, as he moved south, even a short distance of thirty miles, there was less an issue with the 'Geordie' dialect as now he was into a mixture of Wearside, Teesside, Durham and Yorkshire twangs, but it was always important for him to say he was born in Newcastle and he would defend that statement whatever the circumstances and there was never any doubt regarding the pride he had for his birthright. Jimmy Nail's song 'Big River', referring to the River Tyne, "I want you all to know I'm so very proud," is the epitome of Jimmy Bland's feelings.

His own word pronunciations had changed and all the previous few years of derision and scorn were forgotten as he moved on with his life. Until one particular night in Canada, in a Royal Canadian Legion of all places……….. but that's another story.

www.ingramcontent.com/pod-product-compliance
Lightning Source LLC
Chambersburg PA
CBHW030325100526
44592CB00010B/577